Writing a Business Plan Made Simple for Small Businesses and Entrepreneurs

Creating a Template to a Successful Business

Kent Baxter

© **Copyright 2020 - All rights reserved.**

The content contained within this book may not be reproduced, duplicated or transmitted without direct written permission from the author or the publisher.

Under no circumstances will any blame or legal responsibility be held against the publisher, or author, for any damages, reparation, or monetary loss due to the information contained within this book, either directly or indirectly.

Legal Notice:

This book is copyright protected. It is only for personal use. You cannot amend, distribute, sell, use, quote or paraphrase any part, or the content within this book, without the consent of the author or publisher.

Disclaimer Notice:

Please note the information contained within this document is for educational and entertainment purposes only. All effort has been executed to present accurate, up to date, reliable, complete information. No warranties of any kind are declared or implied. Readers acknowledge that the author is not engaged in the rendering of legal, financial, medical or professional advice. The content within this book has been derived from various sources. Please consult a licensed professional before attempting any techniques outlined in this book.

By reading this document, the reader agrees that under no circumstances is the author responsible for any losses, direct or indirect, that are incurred as a result of the use of the information contained within this document, including, but not limited to, errors, omissions, or inaccuracies.

Table of Contents

Introduction

Chapter 1: All About Business Plans
- What Is a Business Plan?
- Why Do You Need a Business Plan?
- Crafting Your Business Plan
  - What Do You Need This Business Plan For?
  - How to Format and Assemble a Business Plan
  - Goals and Company Objectives
  - Using SWOT Analysis
  - Protecting Your Business Idea and Plan

Chapter 2: Executive Summary, Product and/or Service, Customer Base, Competition, and Financing
- Executive Summary
- Main Product(s) and/or Service(s) Described
- Target Customer Base
- Competition
- Financial Projections
- Startup Financing

Chapter 3: Business Overview and Nature of Industry
- Five W's and One H
  - Who?
  - What?
  - When?
  - Where?
  - Why?
  - How?
- Nature of Industry
  - Sales
  - Statistics

- Trends
- Demographics
- How You Fit in the Industry
- Existing Competition

Chapter 4: Market Analysis and Competition
- Direct and Indirect Competition
- Customer Base Analysis
- Analyze Their Marketing Strategy
  - Content Strategy
  - Level of Engagement
  - Promoting Marketing Content
  - Social Media Platforms and Presence
- Competitor SWOT Analysis
- Your Target Market
- The Need for Product
- Estimated Volume of Sales Based on Competitors
- Barriers That Exist and How to Conquer Them

Chapter 5: Sales and Marketing Plan
- Product Offerings
- Pricing
- Distribution
- Advertising
- Social Media

Chapter 6: Management Plan
- Ownership Structure
- Management Team
- Third-Party Requirements
- Human Resources

Chapter 7: Operating Plan
- Strategic Planning
- Production

- Risks
- Facilities
- Staffing
- Equipment
- Supplies
- Industry Affiliation
- Quality Control
- Special Needs

Chapter 8: Financial Plan
- Income Statements
  - Fixed Expenditure
  - Variable Expenditure
- Balance Sheet
  - Assets
  - Liabilities
  - Equity (Value)
- Cash Flow Projections for First Several Years
  - Cash Income
  - Cash Outflow
  - Cash Flow Projection Reconciliation
- Break-Even Analysis
  - Costing
  - Markup
    - Variable Unit Cost
    - Using Data
  - Graphical Analysis

Chapter 9: Appendices and Exhibits
- Business Registration Documents
- Copies of Identity Documents of Business Owners and Shareholders
- Credit History of Owners
- Bank Statements

- Banking Information
- Accountants Information
- Attorneys Information
- Resumes
- Copies of Existing Agreements
- Financial Information
- Building Office Plans
- Letters of Recommendation
- Patents, Trademarks, and Design Registrations
- Marketing Analysis
- Information on Products
- Links to Website
- Brochures or Other Marketing Material Already Produced
- Trade Agreements
- Quotes or Copies of Mortgage, Loans Docs, and Leases
- Other Supporting Material for First Impression

Conclusion
- Your Business Plan and Protecting Your Ideas
- Executive Summary, Product and/or Service, Customer Base, Competition, and Financing
- Clearly Define Your Business and the Nature of Industry
- Market Analysis
- Sales and Marketing Plan
- Management Plan
- Operating Plan
- Financial Plan
- Final Thoughts

References

Introduction

> *"Your work is going to fill a large part of your life, and the only way to be truly satisfied is to do what you believe is a great work. And the only way to do great work is to love what you do."*
>
> ~ Steve Jobs, Co-Founder, Chairman and CEO, Apple

So, you have a brilliant idea or concept for a business, which you're convinced will be a surefire winner. The only problem is that you've been so busy working on product design and sourcing everything you believe necessary for the business that you haven't given much thought to putting a business plan together. You understand how important it is, but your head is so filled with other things that you're not sure where to begin. Yet, your business plan will lay the foundation for the success or failure of your business, so you need to take the leap and get started on it.

This is exactly where *Writing a Business Plan Made Simple For Small Businesses and Entrepreneurs: Creating a Template to a Successful Business* comes in. There's a reason why you've been drawn to this book right now. Whether you're almost ready to launch your product, in the research and design phase, or still considering a side hustle, this no-nonsense guide will provide you all the information you need to put a winning business plan together.

I'm not going to lie to you or mislead you! Right upfront, you need to know that this is going to take a fair amount of work on your part and you will need to be 100 percent committed to do it. Even outsourcing a business plan to save yourself some time, effort, and energy is not a good idea. There are several reasons for this:

- Nobody knows your product and industry like you do.
- Nobody is going to complete this document as passionately as you will.
- By the time you've gone back and forth with all necessary documents to complete your plan, you may as well have done it yourself.

Another important recommendation from the outset is that you don't skip any steps as outlined in the chapters that follow. If they don't apply to your business now, they may later on.

Additionally, if you feel as if you have a good start on your business plan but there's information that you're still waiting on in order to complete it, don't move forward thinking that what you have is good enough. Use this book to put together a complete, solid plan. This is better than submitting a business plan that looks thin on the ground.

Place yourself in the other person's shoes and ask yourself whether you would take "you" seriously with the documented evidence. Most likely not.

You may think that some of the terminology I'm using makes it sound a bit like I'm putting you on trial—and I am in the nicest way possible. Your business is what's on the line. Your business plan will be used in several instances, and it's vital to get it right the first time. Whether you are looking for financial assistance, appealing to investors, providing a pitch to potential customers, looking for business premises, or wanting to apply for relevant licenses or statutory documentation, your business plan will always be the "go-to document."

Once you have carefully crafted this, as per the fool-proof guide in the chapters below, it is a good idea to have several copies printed and bound where they can be easily accessed. An electronic version is also a great idea so it can be attached and submitted to business correspondence when necessary. With any electronic version of important, confidential documents, it is worth either adding a disclaimer or a confidentiality watermark on each page and saving the document in a format that cannot be edited, such as a .pdf file.

Remember that any and all proprietary information, such as trademarks, inventions, or copyright information, should be protected, even in your business plan. For many individuals who have come up with highly profitable ideas and concepts, the reasons for them becoming successful is that their information is protected. This applies to any specific designs, company names, logo, or distinguishing properties belonging to an item.

Many years ago, I was part of a startup run by an extremely successful venture capitalist (who had his fingers in about 16 different businesses). His partner in the business that I was involved in was a young, talented inventor of a unique sports product. The very first thing that was done, before we even moved to what one would refer to as a substantial production run, was to lodge design registrations with patent attorneys. Each time we came across something that needed to be altered or amended, another design registration was filed, and patents were filed for each of the international countries they were thinking of launching in.

At the time we had no concept of how many countries the product would be sold in, but each product that came off the assembly line was covered with the original patent number. We had no ideas at the time that we would end up with 22 different design registrations and patents for most major countries throughout the globe, making it impossible for anyone to infringe on the design of the product.

This is just an example to show how important it is to protect your business or product. The venture capitalist who invested millions in the initial product not only protected his own investment but that of his junior partners as well. This was one of the most important lessons I've ever learned as an entrepreneur. Protect your product, your brand, and your identity. If you do this, you're sure to be off to a good start. It was many months before we even went into production that the product name was even registered along with the design registrations and patents. Don't wait until you're ready to go to market with your idea before you think about protecting it.

As a final note before we get down to the actual business of putting a business plan together, while you are in this phase, you're probably all gung ho and excited about your ideas, your product, and what you want to achieve, but be careful about who you disclose what to! It's better to play your cards very close to your chest until you are covered. Too many valuable ideas are stolen by unscrupulous individuals out there who feel nothing from profiteering from others who are possibly none the wiser. As the old saying goes: "Keep your friends close and your enemies closer." So, be wary of everyone until things are signed, sealed, and delivered.

I'm so excited to be sharing some of the things that I've learned as an entrepreneur and business owner over the last three decades or so. While the business landscape has certainly changed over this time, the fundamentals haven't. Let me help you to put a winning business plan together that covers all the bases and will get you up and running in no time at all. The only commitment from your side is to put all the work in that's necessary.

Let's go build a business plan!

Chapter 1: All About Business Plans

"I knew that if I failed I wouldn't regret that, but I knew the one thing I might regret is not trying."

~ Jeff Bezos, Amazon Founder and CEO

What Is a Business Plan?

You may have heard stories of many successful entrepreneurs who started off their businesses without any documentation or formal business plans. For some, their only plan consisted of a couple of crude drawings scratched on the back of a paper napkin. I can assure you that most of these entrepreneurs became successful as a stroke of luck or what we might refer to as serendipity (being in the right place at the right time.) For the rest of us, not having a plan will more than likely result in impending disaster.

Let me make it quite clear that even with a business plan, there is no guarantee that your startup is going to be a roaring success. Without one, however, your chances of success decrease substantially.

Have you ever had so many ideas in your head simultaneously that you begin feeling confused and unsure of yourself? When there's too much going on and you don't know where to begin? There's a scientific reason for this. According to astrophysicist and scientific writer Clara Moskowitz (2008), the brain is only able to focus on three to four things at a time. This is one of the main reasons for writing your ideas down as quickly as possible, as getting them out of your head allows you to explore other creative ideas. Some of the most creative and inventive individuals always have a journal or notebook handy.

Your business plan should create the entire backbone of your business. Think of it as a spine. If it's solid and secure, it will hold the rest of the "body" of the business in place. Once you have a clear idea of what you want to achieve, it's important to get this down on paper. There's no right way or wrong way to begin this initial process. According to Oxford Languages, a business plan is "a document setting out a business's future objectives and strategies for achieving them." The Entrepreneur Encyclopedia (2019a) provides this additional definition of a business plan: "A written document describing the nature of the business, the sales and marketing strategy, and the financial background, and containing a projected profit and loss statement."

With these two definitions, you will notice that a business plan has various components that cover all aspects of business. A business plan is the path forward for your business. It should act as a GPS, getting you from where you are now (about to begin your business journey) to a destination point (sometime in the future.) By following each of the steps in your business plan, you should achieve the result that you envision for yourself if you've done your homework and have been realistic with all the facts.

In his bestselling book, *The 7 Habits of Highly Effective People,* author Stephen R. Covey (1989/2020) suggests beginning at the end in "Habit 2 Begin with the End in Mind." While Covey refers to the end of your life and creating a eulogy scenario for yourself, this exact principle can be applied to putting your business plan together. Imagine your business two to five years from now and design your plan of how you propose to get there from this point of view. It becomes easier to imagine when you can see the end from the beginning.

This document should be professionally laid out with all the information provided, along with supporting documents where necessary. In the chapters and sections that follow I will provide a clear structure and strategy for you to implement so that you can simplify the task of creating a business plan.

Why Do You Need a Business Plan?

Just as we mentioned that your business plan can act as a GPS, it also provides the *means* for you to get to where you want to be. While having a plan may sound like an obvious requirement for any business, you'd be amazed by how few small businesses or entrepreneurs have one. The lack of a business plan is like trying to build a house without having a set of blueprints. Laying a foundation or deciding where plumbing lines and electrical circuitry need to go could become problematic. Blueprints give you the means for building a house, and you wouldn't dream of trying to build without them. Likewise, any business of substance needs a plan in order to achieve specific objectives.

A plan will allow you to gain a better perspective of what the future may look like for your business. By the time you've completed all your research, you should have a much better idea of the size and scale of your business. By using your business plan, you can identify what's most important to you and your business. It will also help you set priorities for what needs to be done first and by whom. Your plan lets you break business tasks down into manageable goals that are achievable, rather than trying to achieve the impossible in a short period of time.

A business plan can also assist with keeping you on track with tasks that need to be completed on time or within a specific window. There's a phenomenon that's known as "displacement," which is common with small businesses and/or entrepreneurs. This essentially stipulates that when you're only focused on one single thing, it is at the expense of something else. If there's no plan in place, how do you prevent this cost from occurring (Moskowitz, 2008)? You don't.

A business plan can project a growth strategy or can be a means to secure additional funding for your business if you find yourself in financial trouble. This document will be necessary when working closely with other business professionals, such as your financial institution, accountants, attorneys, business partners, venture capitalists, or angel investors. Each of these individuals will need most, if not all, the information contained in a business plan.

To illustrate why a business plan that is agreed upon by all owners is so important, here is a personal story: In 2005, I went into partnership with an ex-colleague, and we were confident that we had "thought" through everything and covered all the bases. We decided to forge ahead with our partnership on a "handshake agreement." We were all enthusiastic to get the business up and running as a matter of urgency and found business premises, signing a 12-month lease agreement. At the time, there were three full-time members of staff. My business partner, me, and a receptionist. We rushed out and registered the business formally with the bulk of expenses coming out of my own pocket on the "agreement" that my business partner would put up their share of what we'd agreed upon.

We focused time, effort, and energy in the wrong direction, because we had no plan. Being exceptionally good at sales and marketing, I went ahead and designed the branding for our business, paid for exterior signage in line with the strip mall we'd chosen to set up shop in. What I learned the hard way is that without the safety net and security of a solid business plan and written agreements, you could stand to lose quite a bit of money.

The buy-in amount we'd agreed to never materialized, the premises we'd chosen to sign a 12-month agreement for became too small for our needs much quicker than anticipated, and little did we realize but we'd picked out offices that were easy for criminals to gain access to. After the second or third break-in and a landlord who refused to do anything to secure the building after hours, it was time for us to wake up and make other arrangements.

Within the first 12-month period, the business grew exponentially (more than we dared to dream initially). If we had a business plan, it's likely we would've chosen a space that fit our projected growth but we had now growth projections. Much larger premises were necessary, but we also needed to be wiser in our business decisions regarding location, such as thinking about passing traffic and accessibility for clients. Once again, no financial input from the "partner" who was enjoying all the benefits of being a named partner on all business documents, all functions and business events, all press releases, and all media coverage.

The second year came and went, all the while the bills began piling up with no financial input from my partner. Sure, they were putting in the hours, as were the rest of the team that we'd grown from the initial three to a total of nine. Then the unspeakable happened: I discovered that my partner was secretly approaching clients behind my back, offering them a discounted rate on our service and was planning on leaving with an entire client base that was two years in the making.

Once again, hindsight is 20/20, and I can see the mistakes I made as clear as day. Trying to get rid of a named partner without damaging your own brand proved to be like walking across a minefield without markers! Removing names from business cards and letterheads was easy enough but restoring reputational damage and winning back the trust of long-term customers took much longer.

Let's just say that this was my personal baptism by fire into the world of small business. And beyond trusting someone I shouldn't have, my biggest mistake was not having a business plan. Without one, my business had many unnecessary expenses that I thought, at the time, were necessary. We bought brand-new assets for the business. This included upmarket office furniture, new computers, and a switchboard and telephone system, which were all purchased brand-new and all paid for with cash. If I'd had a detailed business plan, then I would've understood how much all this new equipment was costing us in terms of our overall budget. I would've understood that we couldn't afford it.

What I was doing was building a house without blueprints and without any clear idea of what I needed and didn't need for construction.

The school of hard knocks and life happened with this business, and by the end of 2008, we were floundering. Business had been particularly bad, and I'd taken my eye off the ball. If I had a solid business plan in place from day one, I would have been able to take this document and present it to financial institutions to back us up financially. Unfortunately, I could not prove that the business had the potential to be profitable once more and that we'd only hit a small stumbling block. Instead of being able to save the business and possibly even selling it to recover my initial investment, all was lost completely.

Life has a funny way of showing you what you could have, would have, and should have done—yet, you didn't! Looking back today, I can't say for certain whether a turnaround strategy could have worked at the time or not. What I do know is that the lack of a solid business plan ended up costing me not only financially but physically and emotionally. I had poured my heart and soul into this business and when it failed, I felt every nail being hammered into the coffin before it was buried.

Crafting Your Business Plan

My main goal throughout this book is to provide you with a step-by-step guide that will help you put a business plan in place that's been drawn up according to best practice standards. While many question whether business plans are still necessary when starting a business, I need to voice a very strong opinion that when it comes to small business and entrepreneurship, the difference between those with a plan versus those without one is like day and night.

Alejandro Cremades, author of *The Art of Startup Fundraising*, confirms that angel investor and venture capitalist David McClure, who has founded more than 500 startups in Silicon Valley, doesn't believe in looking at a business plan. For him, it is all about prototypes and scalability. I guess that when you have as much experience as McClure, it can become second nature knowing whether a piece of tech is going to be the next big thing or not.

Unfortunately, not everyone you're going to meet on your entrepreneurial journey is likely to be another David McClure. This is why you need to put a workable plan in place that will give you the best possible blueprint for your business, and this all starts with your business plan (Cremades, 2018).

What Do You Need This Business Plan For?

So, what are the official steps for setting up a business plan that's going to work? Before you move one inch in the direction of starting your dream startup venture, looking at raising additional capital for your business, finding a new partner, or signing that joint venture agreement, you need to know what the purpose of your business plan is going to be.

For example, are you looking for startup seed funding? Or are you looking for full funding from an angel investor? Funding from a venture capitalist? Or funding from a financial institution? Your business plan should be tailored to your exact needs and goals, and that's why business plans vary from business to business. Knowing what you need your business plan for will give you the context for the layout, language, and length of your document.

How to Format and Assemble a Business Plan

There's no specific format that a business plan needs to take, apart from being laid out professionally with each of the following sections covered (where applicable). Before we go through each of these individually, your "Table of Contents" should look something like this:

Title Page

Table of Contents

Goals and Objectives of the Company

Executive Summary

Mission Statement

Management Information

Description of Product(s) or Service(s)

- Target Customer Base

Competition

- Financial Projections
- Startup Financing

Business Overview

- Nature of Industry (sales, stats, trends, demographics, etc.)
- How Do You Fit in the Industry?
- Market Analysis and Competition
- Who Is the Target Market?
- The Need for Product
- Estimated Volume of Sales Based on Competitors

- Barriers That Exist and How to Conquer Them

Sales and Marketing Plan

- Product Offering
- Pricing
- Distribution
- Advertising
- Social Media

Ownership Structure

- Management Team
- Third Party Required
- Human Resources

Operating Plan

- Production
- Facilities
- Staffing
- Equipment
- Supplies

Financial Plan

- Income Statements
- Balance Sheet
- Cash Flow Projections for First Several Years
- Break-Even Analysis

Appendix and Exhibit

- Credit History of Owners
- Resumes
- Information on Products
- Building Office Plans
- Referrals or Letters of Recommendation
- Links to Website
- Brochures or Other Marketing Material Already Produced
- Quotes or Copies of Mortgage, Loans Docs, Leases, etc.
- Other Supporting Material for First Impression

Covering such diverse information thoroughly and collecting all the relevant data sufficient to put your business plan together is going to take time, effort, and energy.

Because it is so extensive and in-depth, you can feel confident that once covered, there should be no further information necessary.

A couple of important points to remember is that this document is likely to be long enough, so it should be kept as brief and to the point as possible, without adding any additional "padding" or "fluff."

According to Jeff Haden (2018), the author of multiple business and economic books, including *The Transformation Myth*, the reason so many startups fail is because their business plans consist of fantasies. He goes on to say that "you" should be convinced by your business plan and want to invest in your own business. Anything short of this will come across much the same as other business plans: bland, boring, and pie in the sky! Only once your own passion has been ignited will you be prepared to do whatever it takes to make your business profitable and work for you (Haden, 2018).

He also makes some convincing arguments that a business plan is where you begin with your brilliant concept or idea as an entrepreneur or small business owner. Once you see it all on paper in front of you, you may notice that what seemed like a great idea at the time is simply not a viable option for you right now. Not every idea is ready for market, worth pursuing, or a multi-million dollar one (although Haden states that almost every single human being will have **at least one multi-million-dollar idea over the course of their lifetimes**) (Haden, 2016).

The one way that you'll get to discover this for yourself is by stepping back once your plan is in place to gain a better perspective and ascertain the likelihood of success or market appeal for yourself. It's better to discover this now, rather than learning the hard way once you've either invested heavily financially or wasted valuable time and energy.

As we work through each of these sections, we will consider each of the main headings as well as their subheadings so we can begin to flesh out the spine of the business. This flesh consists of facts, figures, and other information that allows us to get to the heart of the business operation to determine whether your idea is viable and actionable or whether it's better to shelve it for another time.

Once you're ready to begin, let's go through each item of the business plan and take note of what needs to be included or excluded when drafting one.

Goals and Company Objectives

Your business plan should indicate predicted growth into the future of your business organization. Questions you need to answer look something like this:

Where do you see your operation in two years from now, five years from now, and even 10 years from now?

As with every new business venture, your business plan should clearly outline where you see your organization going in the future, what you have to offer in terms of either a product or a service, and how you are planning on getting there. Remember how we discussed Stephen Covey's theory of beginning at the end? Project yourself five years into the future and describe what you see.

What's the likelihood of the product(s) or service(s) surviving long term?

This may be difficult to predict if you are launching something unique; however, if your product or service is in a similar niche as something else, make your projections using similar data that's available to you.

Is there room for the organization to grow? What does that growth look like?

How much do you see yourself growing and within what time frame? I mentioned my horrible experience of not working with a business plan, opting instead to "wing it," instead of making wise business decisions. It cost me in the long run because my business's growth was exponential and then hit a slump out of nowhere. A business plan allows you to make contingency plans for these types of scenarios, rather than graduating from the school of hard knocks, battered and bruised!

Where's it likely to take you, and how are you planning on getting there?

Trace your steps from the future point backward until you're once again in the present, marking each step along the way. This will be your best predictor about how you could get to where you are planning on going by using small, consistent steps in the right direction.

Why are you doing what you are doing?

This is probably one of the most vital questions to be asking. According to Simon Sinek (2009/2013) in his groundbreaking work, *Start With Why*, only once you understand why you are doing something does your passion become fully fueled to the point where you can become unstoppable. For Sinek, most individuals understand the "what" and the "how," but they battle to discover the "why." If you don't know why you're doing something, then there's no point in doing it. Especially when it comes to business, without the "why," there's no understanding of what's behind the motivation.

How successful is your business?

This information would pertain to companies that are already trading. It would give potential partners, investors, venture capitalists, and other alliances an indication of your numbers, such as product turnover statistics, average monthly financial cash flow projections, and even unit cost of the product or service you're trading in. Everything in business has a value and a cost attached to it. This cost can be calculated back to actual cost, markups, and profit margins. For any business to be profitable, their income needs to exceed their expenditure. This will be covered in greater detail under the financial information section.

Using SWOT Analysis

Gathering all the information for your business plan can be a time-consuming affair, yet you need as much data as possible to determine whether your operation is worth pursuing. One way to determine this quickly and accurately is by using a SWOT analysis. If you've never been introduced to a SWOT analysis, this is a fairly straightforward, inexpensive tool that can be used to get an overview of what you have going for and against you in your business. SWOT stands for Strengths, Weaknesses, Opportunities, and Threats. By brainstorming under each of these sections, you should be able to gather enough information to tell you whether your business is likely to succeed or fail.

Each section should be distinct and separate. Under each heading, list everything that you can think of that relates to that heading. If you have strengths in communication and sales, include these under "Strengths." If your business is not strategically located, you might want to include this under "Weaknesses."

"Opportunities" might include a competitor being in trouble with rumors in the market that they're likely to go out of business. This would make their entire customer base potential customers for you. "Threats" might include larger organizations that are in the same industry as you.

Once you've completed this analysis, you should be able to step back and confirm whether it is worth chasing this dream or shelving it for a while. One of the most productive ways I've found to get this information out of my head and down on paper is through brainstorming and asking a couple of simple questions each time I discover something new to list under each heading. These questions should include things like: What else? Is there more? Is there something I'm not seeing?

After repeating this process with every single idea that you have, you should have in front of you a fully fleshed out SWOT analysis document. Keep this document somewhere safe because you will be referring to it on a number of occasions as you finish your business plan.

Being able to see this information together may already allow you to see that the odds are stacked against you or you don't have a big enough client base. Or, maybe your competition may be too strong to take on as a small business or solo entrepreneur.

Not all is lost here. You can find ways to adjust. You may be able to tell from your SWOT analysis that you need to lower pricing or look for better product options. You might be ahead of your time in your thinking, and in that case, there's no harm in holding off on your project until the economy or the market is ready for what you have to offer.

Your SWOT analysis should highlight competitors who may be much bigger and stronger than you that can potentially threaten your business success. Determining this through a SWOT analysis could be a little tricky as you don't have actual data to work from. You are also assuming their behavior, rather than knowing exactly how they are going to react. Because of this, you can't be certain whether the threats you've identified are going to be real or not. You will use this same formula later on when you're conducting competitor analysis and figuring out how your business fits in the marketplace.

It's really worthwhile learning the many benefits that a SWOT analysis can have in preparing a business strategy. For example, when Jeff Bezos, founder and CEO of Amazon, first started out with the business in his garage, he did all the work himself. After the first few years in the online bookstore industry, his business was deep in debt and he could have pulled the plug. Other online publishing giants, such as Barnes & Noble, lost golden opportunities when it came to blotting out Amazon from the market. They could have easily bought Bezos out when his business was struggling, but they didn't.

Instead, they didn't see Amazon as a threat at all and left the small enterprise (at the time) alone, underestimating what would shift the market completely in Bezos's favor. What all the other online bookstores lacked was the one thing that Jeff Bezos had in abundance and that was his desire to make his customer experience remarkable!

The point is that your goal with a SWOT analysis doesn't always need to be about an actual physical product. Sure, Amazon is all about selling stuff online; however, the main ethos around the 16-year old organization is keeping its customers happy! When customers are happy, they are loyal, and you can't put a price on that (Bezos, 2020). A SWOT analysis can take things like this into account so that you can build a great business strategy. Or you can be like Barnes & Noble, who likely didn't fit Amazon into their SWOT analysis.

Overall, your SWOT analysis can help you understand the different aspects of your business, what obstacles you might face, the strengths you have, and where your business fits in the larger landscape. All this information will serve you well when embarking on creating your business plan.

Protecting Your Business Idea and Plan

Once you've completed your SWOT analysis and decided that your product and the market are worth pursuing, one of the first things you need to do before discussing concepts, ideas, or services with anyone is to make certain that you are protected. Have anyone and everyone you discuss your concepts with sign a non-disclosure agreement (NDA) while you're in the process of getting all your paperwork in order, such as patents or trademark registrations.

If you're in the service industry, it's a little more complicated than protecting an actual product; however, there are other forms of copyright protection. For example, copyright laws protect authors from having their work plagiarized, and written works can be registered under intellectual property protection.

People can be unscrupulous and some have no problems stealing concepts and ideas from you and then passing these off as their own. It happens all the time, and unless you keep your information guarded and secure, you can find yourself worse off without a leg to stand on.

In the early 2000s, I worked closely alongside a charismatic individual who was highly motivational and said all the right things. At the time, I had been working on a combined project with an educator where we were looking at addressing high unemployment issues through specialized training. I had been totally fooled by this charismatic individual's charm and the way they could capture the hearts and minds of an audience. I decided to approach the business with our training initiative, and we got together for a meal to discuss business. Remember the back of the napkin concept? This is exactly how I took him through our strategy step by step. He made sweeping promises of how and where the concept could be used to address various unemployment and other similar issues at the time.

Together, my writing partner and I waited. Fortunately, my gut instinct kicked in and whenever he called for the actual material, I refused until we had an NDA signed or another contract in writing. We realized that the intellectual property on the information we had was way too valuable and my gut told me not to trust this individual any longer.

Months after our initial meeting, I heard rumblings in the marketplace that he had tried to pass off a training course that had the exact same outcomes as ours to an international corporation. That immediately explained why he was constantly nagging me for a copy of the training material and our business plan. Thank goodness for instincts. When in doubt, always trust your gut, as it will seldom lead you astray. And make sure you protect your business interests and business plan.

So, now, you understand the overall purpose of a business plan, its many parts, and how to format one. You can use the rest of this book to help you build each section of your business plan.

Chapter 2: Executive Summary, Product and/or Service, Customer Base, Competition, and Financing

> *"Good business leaders create a vision, articulate the vision, passionately own the vision, and relentlessly drive it to completion."*
>
> *~ Jack Welch*

Now that you have a business idea and have done the prep work, it's time to get going with your actual business plan. The first step is creating your executive summary. After, you will need to develop sections that delve into what product or service you are offering, who your potential customer base is, what competition you will face, and how you plan to navigate the financial side of starting a business.

Executive Summary

Your executive summary is exactly that: a summary. Think of it as a brief one- or two-page precis of your business. There are a couple of points that you need to include in the executive summary, including:

- a description of the product(s) and/or service(s) you are planning to offer
- an outline of the key objectives you'd like to achieve along with a timeline
- a description of how you see your business landscape

You should also provide a brief outline of your competitors and/or any barriers of entry into the marketplace. Basically, be sure to mention any potential obstacles that you could come up against as you try and launch in a market.

An executive summary should also describe growth potential in the market (current projections) as well as future projections against a specific timeline, such as 6 months, 12 months, 24 months, 5 years, and so on.

You also want to provide a brief overview of the financial resources you currently have at your disposal or the amount of money you will need from other sources. Stipulate possible financial sources, as well, to provide the reader with evidence that you've done your homework.

It's important that your executive summary is not a lengthy or long-winded document. That's why it's called a "summary." It provides the first rough draft or outline of the business blueprint. This creates the first impression for investors, potential business partners, joint venture capitalists, financial institutions, angel investors, and even potential new hires. First impressions need to be lasting impressions, and this is the reason why getting this document right the first time is so important. Even as a one- to two-page document, the summary should outline the whole business so that those who need to make decisions can be fully informed. There should also be enough transparency that they are convinced to become further involved with the business and that the business is worth pursuing.

Remember to include the business value proposition, which is the specific solution that the business is going to provide to the marketplace. Every single business has one of these, whether it's providing the world with the largest online bookstore like Jeff Bezos did or creating the world's first user-friendly computer by linking microchips like Steve Jobs and Steve Wozniak did when they co-founded Apple. But don't think just products, as even offering a service is providing a solution to someone's problem. It's important that you identify yours and that it's included in this document.

Your executive summary should stick to the facts. Watch your language so that you don't go rambling on about things that are irrelevant to the reader of this document. They're looking for facts, figures, and information that they're able to process logically.

Be realistic in your timeline projections. The reason why so many startups or potential startups fail is because they are overconfident with their numbers and underestimate the time it takes to grow a business realistically. Sure, there are exceptions to the rule, but it's better to err on the side of caution with this document.

The best time to write your executive summary is right at the beginning of your startup phase. Because this is only a one- or two-page document, you will already be able to tell after this stage whether you actually have an idea that's worth pursuing or not.

Your executive summary should have the below headings that should then be fleshed out with your ideas. Remember: facts, figures, and brief information only!

Introduction

A brief introduction to the business and what it intends to accomplish within a specific time frame.

Company and Management

All relevant company information, including registration details and information about the management team who will oversee the daily operations of the organization.

Market Opportunities

Information about your specific opportunities within the marketplace. Also, define the size of your market (local, national, or global). A lot of this information will come from your SWOT analysis under the "Strengths" and "Opportunities" sections.

Competitive Advantage

Here, discuss what advantage you have over other organizations. For example, when Steve Jobs and Steve Wozniak started Apple, their aim was to create a personal computer that was more user-friendly than the corporate IBM computers in the marketplace at the time. As a competitor to IBM, they weren't interested in the corporate market. They targeted homes and individuals instead, and everything was user experience focused (Travis, 2018). That strategy was their competitive advantage, and you want to include something unique to your business in this section.

Financial Projections

Financial projections should include ALL startup costs (down to the seemingly trivial things like cleaning products for your office, beverages, food, and even toilet paper). These are things that many startups fail to include in their projections, but someone ends up funding these items for the duration of your startup period. When working on financial projections, you want to set a realistic timeline. If you're seeking funding, look at covering all expenses for the first year of operations in this section and not just for 3 or 6 months.

Mission Statement

A mission statement is usually a two- or three-sentence statement that outlines what the business is all about and what its main purpose is in the industry. It should include your core business, the products that you offer (a broad description), and the geographic location you're operating within. When you begin designing your mission statement, it may be worthwhile to include your staff, management, partners, and any other key stakeholders in the process. Ask everyone to write three sentences that they believe best describes the organization and where they see the business going.

Your mission statement is for your own staff internally, and while it may be shared with customers, its purpose is to motivate your own people to adopt an approach of excellence in everything they do. As time moves on and your organization experiences growth or the business begins heading in another direction, your mission statement may need to be reviewed and revisited again. This should be something that everyone within the organization adopts as part of the organizational culture.

Management

This section should contain all relevant information that relates to the management within the organization. You may want to insert an organogram, which is a graphical organizational chart, to illustrate exactly how each individual fits into the organizational structure. An organogram is typically drawn in landscape format with a top-down structure. So, the organization's founder or CEO is right at the top of the organogram. It should then branch downwards from there, indicating names and specific roles of everyone on the management team. These tiers would include operations, manufacturing, marketing, human resources, and financial. Each of these may or may not have supervisors, team leaders, or junior managers represented in the various departments, which would create more lower tiers.

Depending on your specific business structure, you might not have some tiers or some of these tiers may change to match the needs of your business. If you're a small business or a solo entrepreneur, you may be fulfilling each role for the first while and outsourcing other key functions that you may not possess the skill set for right now, so it is okay to have yourself listed in multiple roles.

Main Product(s) and/or Service(s) Described

After you've completed your executive summary, you will want to describe the main product or service that you will be offering in its own section. This should be a detailed part of your business plan. From start to finish, you need to cover all the bases.

For example, if your business model includes buying products wholesale and adding a profit margin so that you can resell to customers online, then this is what the product description section should describe in detail. Each item should be listed independently with relevant detailed descriptions, dimensions, and specific information. The reason for this is you want to be able to expand or subtract from this list further down the line. If your product is sourced internationally, remember to include how you plan to distribute the products to your customers or end users. If you are offering services, these should be listed in this section of your business plan, too.

You may have multiple products or services that have different end uses. This is where photographs, logos, trademarks, or design registrations should be. You may have different brand names for different products, and these should be neatly arranged along with associated information. This is where you are going to flesh out your business plan so anyone picking it up can immediately identify with the product(s) or service(s) you're offering. Providing as much information as you can, should keep product or service-related questions down to a minimum.

Target Customer Base

The next section of your business plan should consist of a detailed breakdown of your target customer base. This is how you can begin to identify and develop a marketing strategy that will best suit your business. Some of the points you want to cover are:

- who your customers are
- what they are going to do with your product(s) or service(s)
- why they need your product(s) or service(s)
- what solution your product(s) or service(s) provide
- what makes your product(s) or service(s) unique
- what value your product(s) or service(s) add to a customer's life

Competition

Another section of your business plan should present an analysis of your competition. For this section, you will want to answer some, if not all, of the following questions:

- Who is your direct competition?
    - ☐ What do they do?
    - ☐ Where are they situated?
    - ☐ What makes them a threat to you?
- What are they doing to earn the respect or loyalty of their customers?
    - ☐ Is it their brand?
    - ☐ Is their product superior?
- How can you go up against them, especially to achieve some of their market share in the industry?
- What can you do to convince some of their loyal customers to at least try your brand?

Financial Projections

Although you touched on financial projections in your executive summary, you want to build on those ideas in this section of your business plan. Being able to see into the future with financial projections is always something that could be difficult to get 100% correct at all times, but you must do the best you can with the information you have.

We've already mentioned that if you're planning on setting up a fully functioning business, you need to have enough finances available to cover a 6-month window. It really doesn't matter whether you're currently looking at a startup or you've already been in business for a while and you're looking to expand, having a 6-month buffer will help you face slumps that could occur in the marketplace.

In this part of your business plan, you should also be able to predict (as accurately as possible) where you see your business growing within the first 6 months, 12 months, 24 months, and up to 5 years, if at all possible.

While nobody has a crystal ball to make predictions to the last dollar, speak with financial advisors to see where your product is likely to go based on an average to conservative growth pattern. Being cautious is better than being overzealous and providing financial projections that are too good to be true. Remember the adage that if something sounds or looks too good to be true, the chances are that it probably is!

Consider some worst-case scenarios as far as your financial plan is concerned so it is realistic. This is a better strategy than assuming that business will be booming from day one. Maybe you will have similar success as Steve Jobs and Steve Wozniak, turning a couple of million dollars profit in your first year; however, it's probably more likely that you walk a similar path as Jeff Bezos, who had to wait several years before Amazon showed any dividends, proving that even the most profitable, multimillion-dollar ideas and businesses that start in garages can have two different first-year experiences (Travis, 2018; Bezos, 2020). So, try to account for both steady growth and success in this section.

Startup Financing

My number one tip when it comes to this section is to make sure you specify and account for everything that you will need to start your business down to the last paperclip! It is easy to think that you can "wing it" initially and get by with business tools and equipment that you may already have. Once again, I draw on my own personal experience. You have this great idea and want to go it alone as an entrepreneur in a field of business offering a consulting service direct to private individuals or businesses. You can work from home, so there's no expense, right? You already have a laptop, so there's no need to expense for one, right? Your phone is registered in your personal capacity, so there's no need to expense it, right? You can add a host of things to this list to the point where it is rather lengthy and you're fitting the bill for everything. This is where most entrepreneurs make a huge mistake.

Initially, there should be no problem if you are only looking at doing this for a month or so. After this, chances are that good old Murphy is likely to strike and strike hard: Whatever can go wrong, will go wrong. This could be anything from your car breaking down to technology crashing on you. Remember the 6-month financing rule? That buffer of cash in the bank should always be available and should be rotational.

Expense everything. From day one, keep your business and private things completely separate. Even if using your own equipment, set aside a percentage monthly as if you were renting the equipment from a third-party.

Repeat the process for your vehicle: Set aside a fixed amount and expense it for the use of your vehicle, fuel, and wear and tear for business traveling. Keep a logbook in your vehicle for accurate record-keeping and tax purposes at the end of each financial year.

Write everything you are going to need for your business down. Cost items accurately by shopping around. You can do a lot of this online and add a little for wiggle room. If you know that you're going to need to move into office premises with a warehouse for storing stock, consider this from the beginning and phone commercial rental agents for average prices. Add this to your startup costs.

This list should look something like this:

Office Premises

Consider all the variables that will suit your business and go with a midsize average cost. This should be included as a monthly expense unless you are planning on investing in property as a long-term solution. Some other great options would be hiring an office in a shared services suite of offices. These are fully furnished offices that have all the added benefits of conference and meeting rooms and a professional receptionist who can field calls and take messages. You're only paying for the single office suite and whichever shared services you make use of. Whatever your office space, include it in your financing.

Office Furniture

This will be a one-off cost unless you are planning on renting. Rentals can work out more costly in the long term but may be a way to reduce initial startup costs. You can rent office furniture for a single individual and grow from there. If you refer to the shared services above, this would be expensed monthly.

Office Equipment

This includes printers, laptops, servers, computers, and professional equipment necessary to provide the relevant services to your clients.

Transportation/Travel Expenditure

This should include all business-related travel expenditures, such as flights, car rentals, hotel accommodations, and transportation of goods and services.

Stationery and Printing

All stationery costs including branding, advertising, business cards, and publicity materials.

Telephones

All telephone equipment necessary for business operations including calls, internet, Wi-Fi or fiber capability, and data usage.

Cleaning Expenses

Expense for a regular cleaning service to keep your work environment looking neat and professional. This is an advantage to working from a shared service environment. Most of the time, all these services are included.

With your executive summary complete and with the work you've done researching your customers, competition, and projected finances finished, it's time to dive headfirst into all the small exacting details of your business.

Chapter 3: Business Overview and Nature of Industry

"What do you need to start a business? Three simple things: know your product better than anyone, know your customer, and have a burning desire to succeed."

~ Dave Thomas, Wendy's

This section of your business plan will provide a thorough and detailed outline of the business and what you are planning on selling or doing under the banner of your business. If your business is already trading, it is easier to write your business overview section. The reason for this is because you'll simply describe an outline of what your business is currently doing as well as any expansion plans for the future. If you haven't started your business yet, it is more difficult to outline how and what you see your business "becoming" in the future. We will then go over the section of your business plan that we expand on the nature of the industry your business will be functioning in.

Five W's and One H

Some techniques for developing your business overview from scratch is to ask yourself a number of questions for each area of the business. These questions are based on a process known as "five W's and one H," namely:

Who?

Who needs to be involved in the business and in what capacity?

Some examples of who should be included in your business overview are management within the business, key staff members, strategic stakeholders, clients, suppliers, and anyone that has a role to play within the business. If you're in a manufacturing environment, then this would include specialized workers who are involved in the manufacturing process. You might want to include your customers in this list and describe any typical attributes that they might have. All people or parties would fall into this part of the business overview section.

What?

What are your goals within the business against the various timelines? What are you hoping to accomplish with the business or with your product(s) and/or service(s)?

This section covers all your plans for the business and for your product(s) and/or service(s). This should end up being quite a substantial list. Everything under this section would provide an answer to a "what" question. As you answer and list everything that you can think of, keep asking yourself "and?" or "is there more?" This will allow you to do a deep dive into each of these questions while fleshing out the spine of reasons behind your business.

When?

When should you plan for specific things to happen?

This section should focus on your timeline for meeting small and large business goals. As with most things in life, having a plan to work with is much better than having no plan. Your business should be broken down into manageable steps along a timeline so that you know that you are on track or whether you need to adjust your timetables.

An excellent way to work with "when" questions is to use your timeline as a predictive instrument. I have always found that working with three different timelines can make me aware of all sides of the business. What I mean by this is that I work with a very conservative timeline, a current market trends timeline, and an aggressive marketing timeline. This way, you can plan for different contingencies in the market and in your own development. For example, the market might be in a downturn, which means there is less demand for your product, so you would go with the conservative timeline. However, if the market is booming and your product catches on, then the aggressive marketing timeline would make sense to use, as you want to take advantage of the economic climate.

Where?

Where are you planning on operating?

This section discusses the geographical location that is connected to your product(s) and/or service(s). For example, are you planning on operating only within a small geographic location like your town or community? If you were a nail and beauty salon, the answer would be you are operating locally. Other examples may be within larger communities, such as your county, state, or region. This may be providing a consulting service to a specific geographic region in the US. For instance, you may operate only in the Southeast region or the Midwest.

You could also be an online business that operates nationally through a network of delivery options like courier services, but your options are still limited to the size of their network. Last, maybe you're able to operate internationally because you're providing an online service where people can connect to your business at any time of the day or night. Your business runs automatically whether you're around or not. You also have sufficient internet or online support resources available to ensure that you're operating at all times.

Where could also mean a physical location, if you are looking for passing trade customers. This could be anything from opening a boutique style bistro that caters toward a specialized cuisine or a garage that repairs only vehicles that fall under the Ford brand. Maybe you've invested in a franchise, such as Burger King or Wendy's, and location, location, location cannot be overstressed for the guaranteed success of your business. This section should go in-depth about the "where" of your operations.

Why?

Why are you investing your time, energy, money, and effort into this business?

This question is one that Simon Sinek, author and well-known TEDx Talks speaker, would tell you to get to the heart of first. Understanding WHY you want to do something is a lot more important than actually doing something. Getting to the why will give you the confirmation you need that you are on the right path and fueled by passion or will let you know that your business idea is just a passing phase that you don't feel strongly committed to. Once individuals actually understand the amount of work and effort it takes to open a business, they don't always stay the course, because there's too much work involved and so they just quit (Sinek, 2009/2013). Once you explore "why" you want to pursue this business, you will be better prepared to actually make it happen.

How?

How can you get your business off the ground?

Almost as important as discovering the reasons why you feel drawn toward a specific type of business, the "how" is going to provide you with actionable steps that you can take to fulfill your dream. Keep asking the same questions over and over again until you are certain that you have all the answers and an actionable plan in place about how to do things. It's breaking your business goals right down into small actionable, bite-size pieces that you can manage. As much as your business plan is the blueprint or GPS, once you've broken the "how" down, you're close to discovering the step-by-step process to get there.

One of the most important things when it comes to the business overview is that it should provide an outline of the structure of the business in such a way that is easily understandable to whoever is reading your business plan.

Nature of Industry

Another part of your business plan will consist of a section that delves into the nature of the industry your business will operate in. This section may need to be broken down into smaller subheadings or groups that are easier to understand.

If I go all the way back to my role with the first venture capitalist I worked with in the late 1980s, initially our product was only planned for one market. Soon after the initial launch, however, it became apparent that our product offering could potentially be divided into two specific niche markets. The first was the toy sector, and the second was the professional sporting market. This meant that, although some major outlets like Walmart and Costco would be able to carry both junior and professional products, many other smaller niche stores could fall under an either/or category. Drawing clear outlines of what the client looked like was vital so a proper marketing and sales strategy could be put together.

While the toy store market was discovered quite by accident, it affected our marketing and the ways the product was manufactured, packaged, and branded. It was almost as though there were now two distinct products that, while similar in many ways, were completely different. It gave us another point of entry into the marketplace that we had not even considered when we initially began the business.

Discovering there were two specific groups affected the way we targeted each of the two industries and what our marketing was for each. Initially, we used an all-encompassing global approach to launching the product into the marketplace. This was a mistake (which we had to learn the hard way). We had to discover that the two industries were completely different from one another.

The professional sporting market version of the product became recognized as the elite and best of the best brand. This is what everyone aspired to at the end of the day. Our product had a lower price point than similar products, which made it more attractive to those who were looking for a cheaper option or wanted a point of entry to the sport.

Although the toy industry product was almost identical in every way, we scaled it down by cutting back on certain nice-to-haves and produced a smaller, more cost-effective product that could meet the demands of the toy industry. While this wasn't part of the original business plan for the product, it became apparent this was the best strategy after-market launch and being actively involved in one-on-one customer research and feedback.

Like following a roadmap, once we knew that we were actually moving in two different directions simultaneously, it affected everything. We had to process the product in two different ways. Although the main brand was exactly the same and what had been trademarked and patented was the same, one product would move through a unique channel, while the other product had the potential of moving through another. Naturally, bigger chain retailers were able to capitalize and move both products through their stores, but these were often marketed completely differently.

This example is to show that you must be aware of how your product or service functions within the nature of the industry you are in so that you can include it in your business plan. A product for the toy industry will be different than the one for the professional sporting industry. Overall, the nature of your industry will dictate everything from marketing to packaging. But like me, you might find that your business plan has to evolve after you get your business going.

Sales

When you're creating your business plan, it is important to be able to get your figures absolutely right. As in the example above, we were forced to cut costs drastically on the smaller and/or more junior product, while charging a premium price for the professional item. We had to know how far we could go by costing each item out correctly from the get-go, and this was only possible because we had done the initial work in your business plan, so we were able to use that as a guide.

For me, this meant having a very clear understanding of every single component that went into the manufacturing, design, marketing, packaging, branding, and shipment/delivery of the product. While the product was manufactured by a third-party manufacturer that had signed agreements in place, I still understood the cost of producing it. Initially, I spent a lot of my time at their manufacturing facility, getting to know exactly how the product was manufactured, what processes were used, what processes were going to create potential hiccups for us, and even what processes could be reduced or eliminated.

Before we began processing larger orders, we did a trial launch at a trade exhibition and tested the waters. We wanted to judge for ourselves how the market was going to react and get a better understanding of what our sales projections would look like. The initial product run wasn't especially large, which made perfect sense for any venture capitalist who had already invested heavily into design costs, design registrations, global patent costs, raw materials, packaging, transportation, and the initial launch costs—all of this had been done based on the venture capitalist being convinced that this was a unique idea that would be able to make him and the inventors of the product a lot of money.

This was not going to be a short-term solution or get-rich-quick scheme, and starting a business seldom is. So, a word of advice to anyone looking to design and manufacture a brand-new product that nobody has ever seen before: You need nerves of steel and a clear vision to match as well as some very deep pockets.

It could have all gone horribly wrong, and he would have lost millions as part of the scale-up costs. I think I was too young at the time to recognize the risk that was being taken, but I, too, had an unwavering belief that the product would be hugely successful. But projecting your sales shouldn't include the feelings or dreams you have about your potential success. We did the work and took a calculated risk.

When looking to set your sales targets, be sure to take every single expense into consideration. This is easier to do when you're working with a product rather than a service.

A product you can physically see and calculate your cost per item, adding a suitable markup for a profit margin and being able to move on from there. What's important to remember in this scenario is that you need to add additional expenses for raw materials that won't be used until you have actual orders. Each of these depreciates over time, and the longer you're having to store these items, the more money you are potentially losing. Be cognizant of this fact.

Further, you must take unseen factors into consideration. These are things like office rentals, motor vehicles, transportation costs, and imports and exports duties if you are bringing components in to be part of your manufacturing process. If you are paying out wages or salaries for other labor, add these monthly costs toward all your product costs before you add even one cent to the markup of each item. Only once you have your true unit cost per item should you look at adding a reasonable profit margin to your product where it is still affordable to your target market.

Another part of your sales section in your business overview should focus on what your target customer looks like. How do they dress? What type of car do they drive? How old are they? Remember, I mentioned that quite by accident, we ended up with a product being sold through Hasbro and Mattel as part of our kid's line. This was never the intention, but there you have it. There was a market demand that we had to fill, thus we had to understand our kid target customer in order to understand our sales projections.

If you know what your customer looks like, you probably have an idea of whether or not they will be able to afford your product or not. This is a very, very delicate position to be in. Every product needs to be able to turn a profit; otherwise, there's no point in launching into a market. You must trim all unnecessary costs from the product to get your profit margins up and your costs down.

What's most important when it comes to your sales subheading in your business plan (and what your most important takeaway from this section should be) is that you are able to answer the following questions:

- Who are your clients?
- Where are they?
- What do they look like?
- What can they afford?
- Why should they buy from you?

If you can answer these questions, you should be successful in getting your product into the marketplace. Some of these questions may provide you with some very specific answers like it did to us where we accidentally stumbled on a second market. Unfortunately, not everyone is as fortunate as we were. This is one of the reasons for trying to be as unique with your product or brand as possible. Try and come up with something that's going to make people want, and/or need your product.

Statistics

From day one, you want to keep and collect accurate statistical information. This will assist you in rounding out the nature of industry section of your business plan and in understanding the nature of the industry you're in. Statistics can help you add portions to your business plan that back-up your sales predictions or justify why you have a plan to add a product range down the road.

Keeping accurate statistics is vital to the success of any business organization. It lets you know where you stand and how much product you need to be able to move or sell within a specific period of time. If you're sitting with raw materials in a warehouse somewhere, this all has value, but only as long as there are potential sales in the pipeline to keep the wheels of commerce moving. It's being able to sit and analyze all these statistics and crunching the numbers that you can tell whether you're on target or not.

When Mary Kay Ash first founded her cosmetics business in the 1960s, she modeled the business off of a house-and-home company she'd been employed with for a number of years. As a fiercely loyal employee, she became totally disenchanted with them when they consistently promoted males who she'd trained to be her superior. This made her feel worthless in the eyes of her employer, and with just $5,000, which she had been loaned, she began Beauty by Mary Kay.

What she did correctly was model her own brand-new business on the same business model that she'd just walked away from. Possibly, if she was like me, she looked at the data and statistics available to her and saw where she could come up with an improved business plan. While she arranged for product demonstrations in individual's homes based on the party system like her former employer had done, Mary Kay offered a further incentive that the host of the party would receive a free facial. As her business began to grow, she realized that one of the ways to keep individuals loyal and producing regularly was to provide key incentives. Her biggest incentive for top sales personnel was a pink Cadillac (Biography.com Editors, 2017).

Seeing your growth through statistics is what can help you grow and plan in positive ways. For Mary Kay, she saw, through her numbers, the effects that incentives were having. What started in a small warehouse with only nine staff and a handful of creams and lotions that she's bought the rights to with the $5,000 loan has turned into one of the world's largest multilevel marketing beauty brands. Today, as part of her legacy, her business is worth billions of dollars and still continues to function in the same way she intended it to (Biography.com Editors, 2017).

Without an understanding of your data and statistics, you won't be able to tell what's draining your business dry or what deadweight you are carrying around with you. You must study the numbers. Like I said, this valuable information can help add depth and solid evidence to your business plan. If you're bad with crunching numbers and dealing with figures just confuses you further, appoint an accountant that you trust to walk you through your documents.

The most important takeaway from this section, though, is that you should include statistical information or figures in a month-to-month format for 6 to 12 months in your business plan. In some instances, where you are already up and running, it is even worth analyzing information over a 2-year period rather than just months.

Trends

This can be an important area to include in this section, especially if the industry that you're looking to operate in is seasonal. An example of this is if you're looking to open your home as an Airbnb. Obviously, the area you live in has a very distinctive pattern when it comes to tourism or weather, which means you would need to consider those trends because they could affect your business.

Another example would be if you had a bike rental business in a tourist destination. Your business would be affected by the seasons, and maybe you would only be able to operate during the spring, summer, and possibly early fall months because after that there would be snow in the region. With this information, it would mean that you would need to find some other source of income during the non-busy months.

Additionally, your product may fly off the shelves at Christmas time or other seasonal holidays or your industry may be forced to close over the same period due to forced regulations.

Whatever trends are connected with your business, it's key to be able to recognize them and scale up or scale down your business accordingly to accommodate the marketplace and take full advantage of the good times to provide for those times when business may be slower. Remember that most of your costs will remain the same during these slower periods unless you are hiring seasonal labor. You will still need to pay all your operational costs (something we'll discuss in detail in the financial section). You may even be liable for company bonuses at the end of the year, which could place increased pressure on cash flow if your organization has a December shut down period.

Initially, you won't have any idea what these trends look like until you've been in full operation for the first 12 to 24 months. Unfortunately, you won't have an understanding of how your industry reacts at certain times until you live through them. But you can make educated assumptions in your business plan if you are a new business. Or, if you are a current business, you may understand your trends better.

As an example, for our sporting goods item, we were able to rightly assume that we would make record sales over the holiday season and included that in our business plan. For us, this was the busiest time and we were all hands on deck. We even took on added temporary workers to assist during this time. It was not just for the month of December, however. It was for the three months preceding this period. Because we expanded our reach into other global markets, each new country that came on board were placing their orders simultaneously so that stock could be manufactured and shipped to arrive in time for their holiday rush.

Returning to one of my other businesses (the one from 2005), this is an example of not knowing my trends until I lived through them. This business was focused on recruitment and training. According to industry norms, the recruitment industry is dead during mid-November through mid-January. This is because individuals wanting a new job will stay with their current job, waiting for their bonus checks to be paid out in December and using up their leave days. If people resign at this time, they would normally be forced to forfeit their bonuses and be made to work their notice over the holiday period. Very few individuals are interested in doing this, and few HR professionals or hiring managers worked at this time. Ergo, the recruitment industry was extremely quiet.

In the first year of business operations in my partnership, we agreed to keep some skeleton staff available for the business as a means of growing our candidate database with graduates or those who were on leave who found it difficult to make interviews during the other eleven months of the year. We notified all our clients and/or potential clients that we would be open for business and were anticipating two very slow months. What happened next would never have been predicted by me in a million years! In our first December trading, we had our busiest month ever.

What had happened was that because all other recruitment companies were closed for the festive period, we remained open, closing only very briefly for two or three days. Companies that had received resignations from their employees once they'd got their bonuses were keen to make use of the quiet time to actually conduct interviews with potential new hires.

What we anticipated and what actually happened were two completely different things. We had discovered a golden secret, one that we kept for as long as we continued to trade. We rotated leave throughout the year to remain in keeping with regulatory requirements, but we remained open over the supposed slump period of mid-November through mid-January. Year after year, these continued to be some of our most profitable months in the business, and we inevitably gained valuable new clients who continued to remain loyal to the business thereafter. We also revised our business plan to include this newly discovered trend.

Don't be fooled by what might be a trend in your industry or something you perceived as a trend. Analyze the data. It's the only way to identify whether something is a trend or not. Today, there are many different analytical tools available that you can use to see what's most effective. Trends are predictive indicators of how the market is likely to act or react based on past history. It's using what has happened previously to be prepared for what's coming now. You can then add this data into your business plan.

Demographics

A section on demographics is a key component for your nature of industry section because it is going to paint a picture of exactly what your client looks like. Before you even begin creating any form of advertising, packaging, route to market, and even the product itself sometimes, you need to know what your client looks like.

In your business overview, you should be able to include information that answers the following questions about your customer demographics:

- Are they male or female?
- Are they single, married, or in a relationship?
- What is their educational background?
- How old are they?
- What are their likes and dislikes?
- What are their shopping preferences?
- What is their occupation?
- What is their average income?
- What is their income group?
- Where do they hang out physically?
- If they're online, what sites do they visit?
- Where do they stay?
- Do they own a cellphone or other smart device?
- Are they price sensitive?
- Do they prefer brand or quality?

What's the purpose of having this information you may be asking? Well, you're trying to clearly define, refine, and provide as accurate as possible a picture of what your "ideal client" looks like for your business plan.

For example, in your business overview, you want to get specific about your customer. If you're marketing a high-end entertainment game console, then you want to specifically define your customer as males over 30 years old who are in a higher income bracket. The main aim with demographics is to help you understand your customer's place within your specific industry.

This knowledge can also help you refine your future marketing strategy as well. By spending sufficient time on identifying exactly what your consumer demographics are, your advertisements will be spot-on most of the time. It's particularly important if you are working with pay-per-click advertising and when you want to get your message directly to the end user of your product through channels they are using every day. For example, you could invest in internet or YouTube ads that target 30-something males, because you know that's where they are spending their time.

Your demographic profile is a vital part of your business overview that needs to be completed before you put one piece of sales and marketing information together. It will also give you all the data and statistical information you need to know geographically where you should be concentrating your business efforts. Advertising can be set specific to your correct demographic profile through geotagging software so your message gets to the end consumer.

How You Fit in the Industry

In the industry-focused section, you need to also identify exactly where you see yourself fitting into the industry you're planning on operating in. Do you have a product that is completely unique? Or are you offering an alternative option to a solution that's already in the market?

This would once again require studying the landscape of your product market as well as what makes your product offering different, unique, or more attractive to potential customers. Once you've been within a market for long enough, it's fairly easy to understand how you fit in with opposition companies just by completing regular market analysis studies and checking and redefining your marketing mix as part of your demographics model.

If you're just entering the marketplace with a unique product, none of this data will be available to you for the first 12 to 24 months as mentioned earlier. You will need to gather as much of this market intelligence as you can, so you can add to your business plan and use it to support you when planning new things moving forward. Here, it would pay to look at the demographic information for a company that is closely aligned to your own.

Existing Competition

Just as you have relied on statistics and information for each of the above sections of your nature of your industry section, completing an in-depth analysis of who your existing or potential competition is will be a part of understanding where you fit into the marketplace. And this is important information that needs to be in your business plan.

If you're entering the market with a brand-new, unique product offering, find something that's as close to your product as you can and work out how they might negatively impact your business. When thinking about existing competition, it's also worthwhile thinking about new companies that may also enter the market and how these could pose a threat to you.

As you've made a list of your own strengths and weaknesses as an organization, you might also want to put each of your potential competitors through a similar exercise. This will give you better insights into areas where they may be vulnerable, not just for now but also potentially in the future.

Get to know as much about their business and their products as you possibly can. With the amount of access we each have at our fingertips daily by simply conducting a search on the internet, it becomes really simple to gather plenty of data and other important statistical information on your competition directly from their own websites or on the internet itself. Although this may seem like an impossible task, start small within your own location and use keyword searches for companies that do what you do. You will be amazed at how much you are able to discover within a short span of time.

As a caveat: As quickly as you've been able to discover information about your opposition or competitors online, they will be able to do the same for you. It's important that your online image remains as impressive and untarnished as possible. This will keep you ahead of those who are trying their best to destroy you and everything you stand for as an organization.

Now that you know all of the nuances that go into the business overview section and how to present the nature of your industry, you can get started on doing the research and compiling the information you need to complete a detailed outline of your business.

Chapter 4: Market Analysis and Competition

"You shouldn't focus on why you can't do something, which is what most people do. You should focus on why perhaps you can, and be one of the exceptions,"

~ Steve Case, AOL Co-Founder and CEO

Another section of your business plan will focus on market analysis and competition (this section goes more in-depth than other sections where you might've mentioned similar topics). One of the main reasons for conducting specific analysis of what your competition is doing is so that you can make plans for advertising your own product, brand, or service. You need to know what you're up against and one of the ways to do this is by doing in-depth studies on your competition. According to acquisition marketer Christine White (2018), if your last "analysis" of your competitors was a cursory scan over their online media presence, then you are missing out on vital information that is definitely useful in preparing your own marketing strategy.

A market and competition analysis will help you answer questions about who your main competition is, what their business looks like, and which of their products or services you need to be worried about for both the present and the future. For example, you would want to know if your competitor is a large corporate company or a boutique business. You want to know what products they are selling and which ones are closely related to yours. You also want to know what their sales numbers are like. When you understand what they are doing to attract new customers or even to keep their existing customers loyal, you can leverage this information to create a strategy that improves on theirs.

To get a clear understanding of exactly who you're up against, you need to really understand their business. When you're analyzing your competition, you are looking for the following four things:

- opportunities in the market
- trends within the marketplace
- how to access the market quicker to sell more products or services
- where new products and/or services are necessary

Ideally, you should be aiming at identifying and understanding three to four opposition companies. This should give you enough data to work with when coming up with your own strategy. Below are some key points that can guide you through your market analysis.

Direct and Indirect Competition

When you're conducting your competitor analysis for your business plan, you need to look into every single line item that a company or brand sells. While you're doing so, consider the quality of the items they're selling and the similarities or differences between their product offerings. You also want to compare your products to theirs and determine how close a competitor they really are. You might find a potential competitor isn't one after all and can mark them off your list. However, you will also find contenders to conduct a market analysis of.

There are two categories that your competitors could fall within. The first is direct competition—this means that their product operates closely to yours and would warrant close scrutiny and monitoring on a regular basis. Here, you should be concerned about how much market share they currently have and what sort of threat they actually pose to your product and your business. The one good thing about a direct competitor is that they have done most of the heavy lifting regarding actual market research. They have figured out the impact on the market, costs, pricing strategies, and where to position the product in the marketplace. You could very easily follow their business model or marketing mix when you move your product into the marketplace.

An indirect competitor is a business that has a similar product that, nonetheless, has significant differences, so they don't really pose a threat to you or your business. These indirect competitors should still be monitored in case they change or alter their product in a way that turns them into a direct competitor. In this instance, they could become a threat to your business and must be included in the section of your competitor analysis that focuses on direct competition.

To help you understand how to complete a product/service market analysis of your competitors, let's work with the following case study:

You are running a franchise gym and decide that the current rent for your property is exorbitant. Across the way from your current location, a brand-new building with retail space that can be made to measure is being built. Buying one of these storefronts would mean that you would be paying toward your own property, rather than paying rent for someone else's property. You decide to go for it.

Once the building is ready and you've moved, the space that you vacated stands open for a while (no threat to your relocated business), but then a private gym opens in your previous location. Their rates are cheaper than you are currently charging. However, as part of a franchise, you have brand and name recognition.

Do you need to worry about them taking market share from you?

You will only have an idea of the exact impact that this new operation has after a set period of time. In this instance, I would conduct a competitive analysis at 6-month intervals for a period of 2 years to determine whether they will have a positive or negative impact on your business.

To complete the first analysis, you compare your gym business to theirs, including listing all the differences and similarities. For example, what gym equipment do you have that they don't? How many training bikes do you have? How many do they have? What are the differences in personal training? How many personal trainers do they have? Is it less or more than you? What exercise classes do they offer? What do they charge for classes? Is it less or more than your similar classes?

You may need to send someone undercover to discover what they are offering your potential customer base that you're not so that you can include that in your analysis. This also allows you to make whatever changes are necessary in your own business organization to stay in competition. If you were the only gym within a 10-mile radius previously, and now there's a second one that's less than a mile from your new facility, this has the potential to create a problem for you. You will need to keep on upping your game to attract new customers and keep your current market share.

You may find that you lose some customers initially with this new direct competitor. Or, once they've been with the replacement gym for a given period of time, the newness could wear off, leaving these customers less than happy with what they signed up for. You may find these individuals returning to your gym and your numbers once again increasing, making this new gym indirect competition.

While this example may seem overly simplified and easy to replicate (which it actually is), it forms the correct basis for a competitor analysis. You can use this example as a jumping-off point for the competitor analysis section that will go in your business plan.

Customer Base Analysis

As part of your market and competition analysis, you also want to take a look at your customer base compared to your competitors' customer base. You want to know how your competitors have positioned themselves in the marketplace, what their customers typically look like, and how they are selling to those customers (online, through conventional stores, or both).

In the above example, the customers look almost identical. They may have health problems or be battling with obesity. Some may be gearing up for a marathon and want to work with a personal trainer to meet their goals. Ideally, in your competitor analysis, you should be able to identify all of the reasons a customer chooses a specific product or service. There are many key selling points within that information that you can use to promote your business and offer solutions to potential customers.

Remember we mentioned that for any business or service to be successful you need to be able to provide a solution to someone's problem. In modern marketing, these are referred to as pain points. By identifying exactly what your client's pain points are and knowing how you can solve them is key to developing your own marketing strategy that can be pitched directly at your competition's weaknesses. While it may sound ruthless, in business, you are trying to create as much market share as you possibly can. Your market share will directly link you to your business success.

Analyze Their Marketing Strategy

Once you know that your competitors are successful at attracting their customers, you need to analyze their marketing methods. This will then help you understand what similar strategies you can use in your own marketing plan, which would be included in your overall business plan.

In our gym case study from above, you would want to, from the moment the competitor gym opens, monitor what they are doing to recruit new members. Are they offering incentives like a free 2-month trial period, a family-and-friends discount, or a free sport's bag, towel, or water bottle? Are they offering free Body Mass Index (BMI) assessments? What marketing materials are they employing? Are they using local print media like newspaper ads or mailers? Are they printing glossy flyers and handing these out in the mall where they are located? For you to stay on top of their marketing trends, you need to know what they're doing and what sort of impact this is having on their business.

For a product-based business, marketing might look a little different. For example, you've probably been in a grocery store and come across a promotion where you are offered a taste of a new food product that is now available. This is taking a two-pronged approach when it comes to marketing. First, they are creating market awareness of a brand-new product that's just landed on the shelves, and if you think that the young, promoters are simply there to assist you with a taste of the new product, well, they're doing way more than that.

They're actually monitoring your reaction to the product and will complete and submit assessment reports back to the manufacturer/distributor at the end of their shift. They take note whether you come back for a second taste and whether you add the product to your shopping cart. They may even offer you a discount coupon or ask you a couple of questions while you're there. These will always be brief and product-related, but they are gathering valuable market intelligence that will be used to either continue with the product or have it as a limited edition item.

This example is just to show how complex and multilayered a marketing strategy can be and what types of information about a customer can be gathered. When conducting a marketing analysis of your competitor, you are going to want to analyze all aspects of their strategy. For instance, if you discover that in-store taste tests boosted their sales, you would want to work this same strategy into your marketing game plan. Below, we will discuss the different types of marketing concepts you want to consider when putting together your market and competition analysis.

Content Strategy

Content strategy is usually related to what your competitors have to say about their product or service through blogs, videos, whitepapers, infographics, emails, and more. You want to closely examine this content and look at what it says and how it is said. For example, are they making promises or claims in their advertisements? Can these be verified? What language do they use? Are they formal or informal? Has their marketing script been professionally scripted and presented in such a way that it's easy for their potential customers to read and understand? What's included in the fine print? What variety of content do they use? Consider all of these things and make a note of them as part of your marketing analysis.

Level of Engagement

How well your competitors handle their level of engagement with their customers or potential customers will often be directly linked with online marketing. Gone are the days when a business could take the time to carefully and creatively develop and design advertisements to entertain, delight, and speak directly to their customers. Now, you must create ads that can engage customers right where they are, which is online. You have the ability to connect with your direct market via geotagging, to sort through people's unique preferences, likes, dislikes, and shopping habits, and to access a whole host of other demographics.

For a competitor analysis, you must understand how your competitors are engaging with customers through their online marketing methods. It's normally pretty easy for you to follow these ads and monitor the way customers or potential customers react to them.

You also want to analyze the ways in which your competitors interact with customers. For example, in online forums, do they answer questions professionally or are they more evasive or defensive when people ask for specifics? In business, if your customer happens to reach out to you, you want to always enter into a dialogue with them. Don't ignore them because you're too busy with the next biggest thing happening in your business. A low level of engagement by your competitors shows their weaknesses, which you can take advantage of.

Also, how often is your opposition engaging or communicating with their client base? Is it happening daily, weekly, bi-monthly, or monthly? An easy way to check your competitors' engagement is by signing up for their email list. You probably already have several email subscriptions to the businesses, brands, and products you're interested in. You'll notice that some companies send weekly emails while others send daily ones. Well, your engagement with these emails is always monitored so that the sender can analyze what kinds of emails generate the most engagement or clicks.

When it comes to engaging with your customers or potential customers remember to always put your money where your mouth is. If you commit to two emails per month, make certain that you are going to be sending out at least two emails per month! You may notice that your competitor doesn't keep their word. This is a surefire way to lose customer loyalty. You might also notice that your competitor sends a lot of emails, more than they promised, which can be frustrating to customers, who might then feel like they are being bombarded and will hit the unsubscribe button, thus diminishing customer engagement.

There is a fine line between engaging too little and engaging too much, and by understanding how your competitor is engaging with their customers, you can gauge what level of engagement works best for your marketplace.

Promoting Marketing Content

You should look at the different ways that your competitors are promoting their marketing content. If they are local, are they advertising using visual banners and bunting around their business? Are they handing out special offers printed on high-quality materials? Are they mailing out flyers to all the local neighborhoods?

You also want to examine the way they promote themselves in terms of their brand image. Their marketing materials will help you understand how your competitor sees themselves. For instance, do they use fancy fonts and formal language in their flyers? Do they use fun images and witty sayings on their banners? All this can help you center yourself in the marketplace, either following in your competitor's footsteps or branching out to take on a different image.

If you don't believe that image and the way you promote content is important when you're first starting out with your business, I can tell you that you couldn't be more wrong. Big brands are always highly focused on getting their corporate image (CI) 100% correct in absolutely every aspect of their marketing. Businesses spend millions of dollars developing the right image for their product or service. If even the smallest word is off or the wrong color chosen, entire marketing plans can be scrapped, and it is back to the drawing board. It's always worthwhile to develop your brand image and then stick to it consistently. Widely different marketing materials that are promoted in different ways can confuse your customer. You want to promote a distinct, unique identity through all of your marketing efforts.

The way you promote your marketing content should be aligned with your marketplace and your customer. By analyzing what your competitor is doing, you can develop your own marketing content that not only supports your brand but your overall marketing strategy.

Social Media Platforms and Presence

Social media is rapidly becoming the go-to marketing platform for all types of businesses. Even service industry businesses who don't sell an actual product are now relying on the internet and social media to reach clients and potential customers. Chances are your competitors are doing the same, which is why you need to analyze how they use social media in their marketing strategy.

When I refer to social media, I am talking about the five to six most important platforms that include Facebook, Instagram, Twitter, YouTube, LinkedIn, and Pinterest. Each of these has different benefits and appeals to different audiences. Depending on your market and product/service, your competitor may be using one, two, or all of these platforms, which means that you should be using them, too.

Now, it's worth exploring each of these platforms in-depth so that you understand why a competitor may have chosen one platform over another.

With Facebook, you can hone your target market, and for a relatively low fee, you can reach them easily. You can also set your ad spend so you're not going to go over budget. Another huge benefit of Facebook is that you can monitor the analytics to see where your ads are performing better. This allows you a whole host of variable analytics to choose from to further refine your ads.

Owned by Facebook, Instagram is mostly a platform that is used for sharing visual images. It has a similar ad structure to Facebook where you can target potential customers so that they see your post. Instagram is a great tool for building your brand and image as you can curate the photos you post and write captions that encourage customers to engage with you.

Twitter gives you access to a global market and is a great avenue for generating a loyal customer base through interactions. You can reply, tweet, and generally hold conversations with your customers through the platform. It also allows you to use targeted ads like Facebook does so that you can reach a specific audience. Similar to Facebook, as well, you can track your analytics and engagement in order to refine your marketing approach.

YouTube can also allow you to reach a global audience. You have the freedom of being able to post almost anything creative on YouTube from the mundane to the ridiculous. If you have a product that needs demonstrating, consider using YouTube as an interactive way to explain how your product works through a demo or by hiring someone to review it. There are many individuals and companies that have not only become extremely popular but have readily made their mark on YouTube by creating engaging content that leads to thousands upon thousands of followers. YouTube also allows you to target ads so that you can reach new audiences.

LinkedIn is mostly a professional website that still has some good functions for advertising, interacting, and creating a community. If you are a serious business, you can use LinkedIn to build a professional image by posting content related to your products or services.

Another site that has become extremely popular for sharing things, creating posts, and even running websites from is Pinterest. Here, you can find almost anything you're looking for as a result of the number of different ideas and concepts uploaded to the site by its users. As a business, you can use Pinterest to curate your image or brand by posting relevant content or examples of your products.

The only issue or warning that should accompany working with Pinterest is that none of your ideas are protected. In other words, you could be using the site to promote a totally unique product and would no doubt have paid for professional images to be created and designed to be uploaded onto the site. Yet once uploaded, your images, concepts, and ideas automatically belong to Pinterest, and they can do with them what they will, despite you having all the correct copyright or trademark protection in place. It's best to not open a unique idea to a site such as this one if you know there is even the slightest chance that your intellectual property, trademarks, or copyrights are not going to be safe.

Within your own market and competition analysis, you are going to want to look at the platforms where your competitors are most active. Likely, they have already figured out which social media avenues work best for them and which they get the most engagement on. You can then follow suit to pursue advertising on those platforms and create your own social media presence.

When analyzing your competitor's marketing strategy, you want to consider their content, their level of engagement, the way they promote themselves, and how they use social media to their advantage. By knowing all of this, you are in better shape when developing your own marketing strategy and writing the market and competition analysis section of your business plan.

Competitor SWOT Analysis

Having completed your own SWOT analysis for your executive summary and your business plan, you likely know how useful it is. Well, this same technique can give you a much better understanding of your competition and help you further develop the market analysis and competition part of your business plan.

First, begin by considering your competitor's strengths. This will include an analysis of their products, their marketing, or their branding. Whatever they are doing well, note it here.

Next, consider all their weaknesses. This could be anything from lengthy stock turnaround times to poor customer service. Another way to gather this information is by searching for customer satisfaction information on review sites or at the Better Business Bureau website. This should provide you with enough information on what your competitor is doing right and where they need to improve to meet the demands of their customers. Each of these weaknesses is a potential opportunity for you to replace that segment of their business with one of your own.

Third, look out for areas of opportunities that you can capitalize on when it comes to your competition. You need to be able to leverage your full potential and all the information you have so far gathered about your competition. You should also consider all the opportunities that are open and available to you as a result of errors that they're making. One of the most important things that you need to do when opportunities present themselves is to act on them. If you allow these to slip past you when they're available, then there's no point in getting upset if you lose market share back to them or to another party who also happens to be looking for opportunities into the marketplace.

To the opportunity section, add things like gaps in their marketing content or interaction and how you can employ a better strategy. Being able to recognize and act on opportunities means that you need to constantly have your finger on the pulse of whatever is happening around you all the time.

Be just as open and honest about the threats that might be out there. As mentioned above, probably one of the greatest threats would be another competitor who has recognized exactly the same opportunity and happens to react to it quicker than you did. These threats are more dangerous than having a global threat under one umbrella. New threats mean that there are other players looking to enter the marketplace. You'd rather be dealing with the threat that you know and understand, rather than having to review and begin an entirely new competitor market analysis with new players in the industry.

Your Target Market

Your market and competition analysis needs to also identify who your target market is for your marketing mix and advertising so you can be certain that the marketing messages you send out are specific to them. Something that's become more apparent over the last twenty to thirty years in marketing is that the consumer has changed. You cannot expect something that worked thirty years ago to still be appropriate today. Sure, some of the basics will never change; however, consumers today expect a level personalization that past consumers didn't.

You need to be aware of who you are trying to appeal to and then craft your message specifically to them. Write down every single parameter relevant to your market. Review the previous chapter's section on demographics to remind yourself about all the individuals you've already identified. All you need to do now is to fine-tune your marketing message to suit them and their needs exactly.

You'll want to know what they are interested in, where they get their information, what trends excite them, what social media they use, how much they buy in your market, and what exactly is speaking to them at this specific moment of time. By developing your target market, you are one step closer to business success.

The Need for Product

Another part of your market analysis will be a section that concerns the need for your product. This often speaks to supply and demand, which are economic and manufacturing factors. If you don't know how many products your customers consume on average and how these needs are influenced, it's very difficult to put any worthwhile strategy in place specifically to meet these needs. There's often a discrepancy between the manufacturing department and the sales and marketing department when it comes to getting these consumer needs forecasts correct. One of the reasons this is so important is that if your manufacturing or supply turnaround times are too long, the customer is going to be going elsewhere.

Why is it important for you to get to know and understand who your customers are and what their specific needs are? Without understanding what's driving your customer or what motivates them to buy your product, you are never going to get the solution right.

Are you working to satisfy a basic need such as food, drink, basic clothing, or shelter? If you know Maslow's Hierarchy of Needs, these would be all the essential items at the bottom of the pyramid structure. Customers are looking for products or services that serve a specific purpose or satisfy a need. Your product should make the customer's life easier, rather than more complicated.

Think about the early days when television was first invented. Businesses saw opportunities to fulfill needs in connection with watching television. Thus, came TV dinners. These were quick and easy meals that were specifically packaged and sold for one person. They could be conveniently heated and served simply by removing a piece of cardboard. These presented an excellent solution for eating dinner and watching television at the same time.

With this example, a part of the business plan would be an explanation of how a TV dinner solved the problem of a person not wanting to miss their favorite television show or miss their dinner. While maybe a silly example, it helps you understand how to position your own product or service within the solution category.

Estimated Volume of Sales Based on Competitors

Next, your market and competition analysis should include a sales forecast, especially when your business will depend on manufacturing, importing, stocking, or placing orders for raw materials (as you need to know when to do a certain task or how much of a material you need). Depending on the nature of your business, having a sales forecast to work from is your initial springboard toward earning profits (which is the reason behind every business). To accurately forecast, you need an initial set of numbers or statistics to work from, which could include estimates from sales representatives for orders already placed or call center agents who are in constant contact with your end user or consumer who wants to buy your product.

Getting accurate numbers can be tricky if you are a new business that is about to launch a product. Please accept and understand that your first 3 to 6 months are going to be a bit of a hit-and-miss scenario until you can get some accurate historical data behind you to see how the product is actually performing in the marketplace.

If you don't have your own numbers to turn to, the best place to start to predict future trends is by looking at what has happened in the past with your marketplace or competitors. As far back as you can, look for historical trends and analyze what changes have taken place in the marketplace. This will allow you to see whether these trends are likely to turn upward or downward in the future.

Chances are you're never going to get this 100% accurate, but any good business plan will offer some predictions about how well their product or service will do in the market. This is important information that investors or financial institutions look for when deciding whether they want to do business with you or not.

Barriers That Exist and How to Conquer Them

This is the last section that you need to analyze when you're completing a competitor analysis for your business plan. These are barriers that exist to entering the marketplace. Some of these may be that you're a micro-enterprise or a solo entrepreneur (and large organizations are nervous about doing business with small operations). This is a very real scenario that exists. When I opened my recruitment and training organization, I already had around 16 years of recruitment and management consulting expertise under my belt, but it still took considerable convincing to crack into larger blue chip companies. Once there, long-term loyalty was assured, and while this has not been my core business for many years, I can still reach out to each and every one of my contacts in my network from all those years ago.

The secret to sales and creating a successful business organization is building it on trust and being the kind of person that people like, trust, and want to be doing business with. While trust could be an initial barrier, it can be overcome and be turned into lifelong loyalty.

Other barriers to entry are capacity. You may only be able to manufacture or produce a certain amount per month; however, there are ways around these limits. When we originally started with our sporting goods product in the late 1980s, there were agreements put in place with a third-party manufacturing company. They had the capacity that we lacked, and if the project failed, neither organization would be badly out of pocket. As the owner of the brand and designer of the product, we paid for all the molds required to manufacture the product, and we absorbed all raw material costs as well. The only expense the third-party manufacturer was carrying was machining time and some labor costs, which we were ultimately picking up.

Once we knew where we were going with this product, this manufacturer had to work extremely closely with us, making alterations, and coming up with different designs and models as the product rapidly morphed along with the trends and requirements from the marketplace. Fortunately, I had an exceptional working relationship with them, and we were able to meet all requirements without too many barriers to entry in the marketplace.

We could have faced barriers getting into larger chains like Walmart and Costco; however, at the time, the venture capitalist was already a key supplier through many of the other products and businesses that were already registered as existing suppliers. Yes, this meant making new contacts in each of the buying departments that represented sporting goods but what could have been monumental obstacles to overcome, ended up being smaller, smoother pebbles that were easy to step over.

All of that is to say that you must see your entry barriers as they are and be realistic about them. However, that doesn't mean you accept that they will always be there. A good business plan will account for entry barriers and offer solutions on how to overcome them.

In the end, your market and competition analysis section will be a detailed, complex document that accounts for things like your direct and indirect competition, the marketing strategy of your competitors, market conditions, and how your business fits into the larger picture.

Chapter 5: Sales and Marketing Plan

> *"If you are not embarrassed by the first version of your product you've launched too late."*
>
> ~ Reid Hoffman, LinkedIn Co-founder and Venture Capitalist

Although sales and marketing are mainly used together and come across as being a single entity of the business plan document, they should actually be separated into two different groups. There's nothing wrong with having a common goal when it comes to market share or sales that you want to achieve, but understanding that each of these is different parts of your business plan is a step in the right direction.

Your marketing plan describes who your customers are, what they look like, and where they hang out. Your marketing plan is all about identifying them and the best way to get your products to these customers. This becomes your how-to document when you're looking to increase market share in the industry and reach those in your customer base that you've managed to identify. It's the strategy that you'll put together to get the word out in the marketplace that you have a product that the customer wants or needs to make their lives easier.

Your sales plan, on the other hand, will describe in detail your sales process and how you plan to sell your product to your customer, client, or consumer. It's a completely different document that outlines your actual sales targets in numbers. These are the actual goals. You want to sell "x" amount of product within the next 3 months and "x" amount of products by 6 months. Your marketing plan usually provides you the how of making those sales goals. It's what you need to accomplish for your business to be profitable and succeed.

According to R. L. Adams (2017), entrepreneur and founder of Wunderlustworker.com, too many business owners or entrepreneurs are so busy working in their businesses that they are not spending enough time on their businesses. What he means is that they're so focused on the smaller issues at hand that they miss out on the big picture. The solution is to step back from the business so you can get a better view of things from a distance.

None of us enjoy failure. It's probably one of the worst feelings in the world, especially when it comes to failing in business, so what can you do to prevent this from happening? Or what strategies could you implement to minimize the fallout?

Adams (2017) makes the very valid point that what's worked well in the past has no guarantee to continue working again in the future. This is applicable in an ever-changing world and society that we live in where people are demanding better and better all the time. They want their products to be high quality, functional, and at the best possible price. Anyone in the marketing industry will likely tell you exactly the same thing: Trying to get each of these three areas to balance is a major juggling act. It's not impossible to accomplish, but it does take work.

For your sales and marketing strategies to be effective, you need to be working on plans and goals that are realistic and achievable. There has to be both incentive and reward if you are relying on staff members to grow your business for you, even when they're employed specifically in a sales or marketing capacity. While this is ultimately their job that they're being paid for, there's no harm in offering some additional incentives for reaching targets or achieving specific goals and objectives on a regular basis.

These rewards don't even need to be large ones. Sometimes something as simple as a certificate printed in recognition of their achievements can go a long way to making them feel special and appreciated, spurring them on to achieve even more in the following month. There's also nothing wrong with some other healthy competition within your ranks of the organization. Where one person may have achieved record numbers with sales in one month, someone else may feel inclined to challenge them in the new month, going out of their way to do even better.

As we move onto the next sections of your sales and marketing plan, you need to think about what's commonly referred to in marketing as the 4 P's, which stand for product, price, placement (also referred to as distribution), and promotion. You can use these as a guide for developing the sales and marketing section of your business plan.

Product Offerings

The first part of your sales section in your business plan will center on your product offerings. You should include the variety of products you're planning on taking to market and present them in the best way possible. If you have one product, then your job is easier. However, if you have multiple products, group those products together that are closely aligned with one another.

For example, the venture capitalist that I worked with in the 1980s had a company that dealt in food products, toiletries, sugars, and teas. If you have a similar range of goods, then in your business plan, you would want to arrange products into similar categories. You most certainly wouldn't put food products together with toiletries. In most instances, these would be different buyers in large chains. You may get it right to group the food products along with the sugars and teas, because these all speak to food products or consumables that can be eaten and have a shorter shelf life than toiletries, such as soaps and deodorants might have.

From the beginning of your business, allocate similar product groups under the same heading on your initial balance sheet and business plan when you're setting up your business while keeping those that are different under their own product headings. If you know that you're planning on expanding your product range at all, mention that fact in this section as well. Mixing everything under one heading can become extremely confusing to those reading your business plan. Separating them also makes it easier to understand how they will be discussed in your marketing plan section.

In the products section, you also may want to include any information about product testing. Before you can take a product to market, it needs to be tried and tested. If you're asking someone to invest a lot of money into something you haven't defined or tested properly, they might just laugh in your face, and they're certainly not going to give you that money at all. You need to provide some form of proof that you've made an effort to get the product as far as you can.

As an example, Steve Jobs was always focused on user experience. Before doing anything related to design with Steve Wozniak, they were focused on their products being functional and creating the best possible user experience possible. Jobs said, "You've got to start with the customer experience and work backwards to the technology. You can't start with the technology and try to figure out where I can sell it" (Fersht, 2020).

As you can see, they did the work of refining their product before putting it on the market. As Apple grew, they continued to refine and reinvent their products. In order to stay ahead of the curve, they had to rely very much on what their consumers were saying about their products and how they experienced them. This meant connecting the design teams directly to the consumers and formulating focus groups where products could be tested by consumers who could then report back to the design team. The brilliance of this kind of strategy is that you can iron out any possible design flaws to come up with a product that has been honed and finely tweaked already (Travis, 2018).

We approached the market in a similar way for the 1980s sporting goods company. Because the product was so unique and different from anything else available on the market, there was a learning curve that needed to take place before you could physically use the product. Essentially, what we did was create a group of users, taught them how the product worked, provided them with the product, and set them loose on the streets. We met with them regularly for feedback sessions and had an open-door policy that if there were any defects or if the product broke, they needed to meet with us immediately so we could determine what course of action we needed to take.

We analyzed whether each damaged item was due to negligence or poor quality. Each and every time this occurred, we strategized and completed surveys with our team. We sat in endless meetings, going over defect after defect until we reinforced the design substantially. This process took a couple of months to get to the point where we were satisfied that we had a product that would pass all the quality checks we gave it. By streamlining, strengthening, modifying the design, and changing the actual raw material used in the manufacturing process, we were able to create a product we were happy to put a guarantee on.

What I want you to take away from these two examples is that you must always be working to test and refine your product for the market. Your process for doing so is an important part of your business plan. If you run any test groups like we did, include that information and the results in your plan. Show potential investors your exact process for creating your product so that it has become the best it can be. That way, you will be showing your dedication, expertise, and work ethic, which makes you a valuable business partner.

Pricing

This section should include your detailed pricing strategy, and you need to ensure that you've taken all aspects of pricing into consideration. If you're missing information or forget one aspect, then your business plan will suffer for it. First, you must consider the cost of your materials, labor, and production. Yet, when you're physically costing your products out, you need to take all of your costs into consideration. And by "all," I really mean ALL COSTS. Where many companies or entrepreneurs fail is that they forget to add the small costs into their pricing or maybe they think one cost is too small to be considered. But you need to account for each penny. For example, add in travel costs, petty cash, stationery supplies, office cleaning, and technology costs into your product pricing. This may seem silly; however, they are very real costs and need to be covered from somewhere. As the business owner or entrepreneur, you may feel that it is your duty to keep supplying these costs. This is not so, and once your business is up and running correctly, these unwritten expenses need to be included in the unit cost per item.

Further, you also want to include other costs, such as media or advertising, printing and packaging, and any other marketing-related costs that you may not have included as part of your marketing mix. When you're working alongside large chains and you'd like your brand or your product to be strategically positioned in the store so that you have maximum exposure, this is another cost to include. Prime real estate on shelves is always going to cost more than regular shelf space (and yes, you pay for shelf space at certain stores).

Include all of these costs to get to your baseline unit cost. Only once you have this actual unit cost should you look at various profit margins. When working with prices and costs, remember that you are in business to make money! If your product becomes too expensive for your target audience, then you may need to try and find another niche. Alternately, you may need to rebrand or repackage to appeal to an audience that has more disposable income. In other words, they can afford to pay extra for the product.

The other alternative is to make your product cheaper. Here, you would need to, once again, do a complete product analysis to see what you can do away with and possibly where you can cut costs. This could be anything from the way you market the product to how you package the product. You might even reconsider the raw materials used to make the product.

Next, after pricing your product, your business plan should discuss other aspects of your pricing strategy or explain any nuances of your strategy.

To show you one type of pricing strategy that you could use and put in your business plan, let's talk about a discount pricing strategy, which is especially useful when you need a constant cash flow in your business. A lot of major chains don't like to pay on delivery or within a short time frame and will push suppliers off to 90 to 120 days plus before paying their invoices.

For small businesses, this could be the difference between scraping by and going out of business. If this is the case for your business, your pricing strategy would include settlement discounts, which is where you offer a company a discount if they pay their invoice early. Your discount offering doesn't need to be huge, either. Many clients are happy with a 5-7% discount offering. Others may try and push for 10%. Decide upfront how low you're prepared to go and then make certain that you stick to honoring these agreements. You then include the discounted sum in another part of your pricing. For example, you could already plan to add the discounted sum in the price of production, so you're actually not out of pocket at all and are getting paid early.

This is just one example of the type of pricing strategy that you would want to employ in business and include in your business plan so that investors know that you have a keen and workable pricing strategy.

Distribution

The next part of your sales and marketing plan will center on distribution. Basically, this section covers how you plan on getting your product from wherever it is now (warehouse, your business front, or the manufacturer) to your customer. You will need to define what distribution channels you plan on using, including information about how and why they are cost-effective and beneficial to you. You should also keep in mind that looking at the most cost-effective (cheap) means to distribute your products is not always the answer, and sometimes, this can go horribly wrong, leaving you out of pocket and possibly causing you to lose a client or customer.

As one of the 4 P's of the marketing mix, this "P" would actually represent "placement." In other words, it's how you get your product from one place to another. To decide on the right type of distribution channel, you need to consider your product and the type of business you are running.

For example, perhaps, in your business, you will be dealing with your customers directly. This would mean that you have a physical address or an office where you sell your products directly to the consumers or customers. They would approach you for the product, and much of your distribution depends on passing traffic or customers that have heard of you through word of mouth, referrals, or through any of the forms of advertising materials you are using. Examples of this kind of business would include a nail and hair salon that is located strategically in a strip mall in Southern California. There, they would offer beauty services but might also sell hair care products at their location.

Another type of business, which is similar in terms of market and industry but would need to distribute products differently, would be an online shop that sells all-natural beauty products, such as shampoos and conditioners. This business model would mean that they have no storefront for which they can sell products like a brick-and-mortar hair salon does. Instead, this business would need to have a distribution channel that includes getting their products directly to their customers through shipping means. That would entail having a warehouse or another space where orders could be packaged and sent out to the customer's home.

A third option for a business in the same industry would be one where you are a franchisee who sells different types of beauty products, such as shampoos, nail polishes, skin creams, and much more (think the Mary Kay business model). In this case, you would never physically have the products you are selling, just samples of them. The distribution would be taken care of by your parent company and would be a part of a larger network.

So, what that means for you is that your plan for distribution will depend on the type of business you are and the type of product you are offering. You may want to consider some of the following different ways to get your product directly to your consumers, including:

- wholesale distribution directly onto a reseller
- direct sales where customers can place orders directly with you via the internet or your website
- direct sales to customers via an external sales team

Depending on how you decide to distribute your products, you may need to look at several different distribution strategies and include each one in your business plan.

If you are marketing locally within your geographical location where you may have the means to deliver direct to the consumer, you may choose to consider door-to-door courier services (similar to Amazon).

If you're distributing bulk orders, these may need to be shipped via sea or air freight. This means working closely with sea or air freight specialists who know all about tariff codes and headings for imports or export duties, as well as how long it will take for products to be manufactured and transported. The estimated time it will be held up in customs within the destination country and expected time of arrival (ETA) should also be factored in. When running this type of business, it is best to be up-front and honest with your customers so they don't have unrealistic expectations regarding delivery.

Even when making use of local courier or delivery services, take their worst anticipated delivery and communicate this right to your client. For example, if your courier service promises a 5- to 7-day delivery time, advertise your delivery time as 7 to 10 days instead. Remember that it is better to under promise and over deliver than promise too much and disappoint a customer.

To conclude this section, remember that you should include a detailed breakdown of how you plan to get your product to your customer. After all, what's the good in having a product to sell, if you have no way of getting it into a customer's hand? Your business plan needs a well-thought strategy that takes into account all aspects of distribution.

Advertising

Another of the four P's is promotion (or advertising), which is anything that has to do with promoting your product to the consumer. Sometimes, the best way to gather the information needed to create this section of the marketing plan is through conducting regular customer surveys or feedback sessions (like Apple does, remember?). A lot of companies have chosen to go with focus groups to see what works best as far as advertising is concerned. The reason for this is there is no point in spending money on advertising that doesn't work. To get your advertising right, ask those who it influences most of all: the end user.

Should you be manufacturing or distributing any item that is bound by any regulations, make certain that your advertising and packaging complies with all of these requirements. Some 25 to 30 years ago, I was acting as a consultant to a large international agricultural chemical company, working specifically with their marketing team. The company carried approximately 50 to 100 different brands with more than 300 line items when you considered their different size options. Some of their products were manufactured on-site, while other products were shipped from a holding company in France.

As far as regulatory compliance was concerned, each product needed to be referenced and registered appropriately. Every advertisement needed to carry the correct disclaimers and/or proprietary information that related back to the products, their active ingredients, whether they were harmful, and how they needed to be stored. When designing your advertising, you must take this into consideration and include it in your business plan.

Advertising covers so much more than packaging and print. It is being able to manage your main brand at all times and keeping it on point with trends happening in the marketplace. This is fairly easy to do if you have a dedicated sales and marketing professional on board (or even an independent third-party that you contract in whenever necessary). Many companies and smaller organizations retain the services of marketing and advertising professionals on a freelance basis.

If you are going this route, you want to ensure you include this in your business plan. For example, you might plan on finding talented individuals on sites such as Upwork, Craigslist, Fiverr, Simply Hired, PeoplePerHour, or Hireable. These are just a few that can be found on the internet, and naturally, depending on what you are looking for, there may be loads of other specialist sites out there.

Using these sites can be pretty straightforward. You simply post an ad for exactly what you're looking for and wait for interested freelancers to respond. Once you've received a response, you have the opportunity of going through their work samples, conducting an interview with them, or requesting them to submit a specific sample before hiring them to do work for you.

In your business plan, specify the timeline for these freelance hires. It's possible to hire freelancers for specific projects or for 3, 6, or 12 months at a time. Obviously, longer terms cost more in the long run, but relationships are built. You are able to trust the freelancer with more responsibilities if you're happy with the quality of their work. You can also look for a new one when you want to change your advertising direction.

One of the benefits you can add to your advertising section about freelancers is that the control remains with you throughout the entire process. You can set milestones to break larger projects down, which incentivizes the freelancer to put in the extra effort to get your work finished much quicker and get it back to you. Other benefits are that you can find them at a fairly short notice, rather than having to work through a lengthy hiring process and then being stuck with a permanent hire that you may not need full-time at the moment.

Your advertising plan should also consider seasonal or popular promotional elements. For instance, seasonal color trends and current fonts that are on the nose versus old, dated designs. In your business plan, you also want to include a copy of your logo and information about its unique design. This is important because you will be using this logo in all of your promotional materials. All of your advertising also needs a notice or description that the artwork, logo, or design are proprietary information or your own intellectual property, as this way individuals will be less likely to want to rip-off your ideas.

Having all this advertising information in your business plan shows that you have a well-thought plan and strategy. It also will inform potential investors that you have taken into consideration the many parts and pieces that go along with promoting your business or product.

Social Media

Your sales and marketing plan should also include a section that touches on how you plan to use social media. Luckily, you've already done the research into your competitor's use of social media, so you have a head start on creating this section.

In your social media marketing plan, you should have all the facts, figures, and information handy about your budget and strategy. For example, include your total budget for social media advertising broken down into your monthly search engine optimization (SEO) costs, your online ads, and any other content marketing costs.

You also want to include a plan for who will run your social media platforms and strategy. The same graphic designer or freelance artist that you use for creating your advertising materials can be used to set up and possibly even run your social media campaigns as they form part of your marketing mix.

We've already gone through the different social media platforms in the above chapter, and here is where you want to state the platforms that best suit you and your business. Ask yourself which sites your customers would likely be using and how you make your presence known on each of these sites.

If your current marketing strategy is not specialized with SEO or pay-per-click (PPC) advertising, then it may be time to make a plan for expanding into these areas. Remember, I've given you a list of freelance sites where you can find exactly the type of expert you need. If you're currently a startup, I would include this into your plan so that you have a clear idea of what you're going to end up spending on the ideal person, and I would try and go the professional route from the outset.

In today's marketing world, social media is not just a nice-to-have; instead, it is an essential item that should be part of your marketing and business plan along with sections on your products, pricing, distribution, and advertising.

Chapter 6: Management Plan

"The secret to successful hiring is this: look for the people who want to change the world."

~ Marc Benioff, Salesforce CEO

The management plan is an important part of your business plan, especially if you're looking for startup funding from any financial institution or other financiers. This is the plan that details who's who in the organizational structure. It describes in detail what their roles and responsibilities in the business are. This section allows you to highlight specific qualifications that strategic individuals in the organization have and/or the reasons why you hired them in the first place. For some business plans, this doesn't need to be a lengthy document and you could get away with only a few sentences. For others, it will need to be a substantial document. The reason being is that those getting into business with you are looking for a professional document that validates you, your qualifications, and those who are working with you in your organization.

The importance of this plan cannot be overstated because this is where you can highlight your experience as an entrepreneur. If you were successful at inventing something when you were still in high school and have gone on to found and be successful with various different startups, then this is what any financier wants to see. This part of the business plan should sell you in such a positive light that they are almost certain to sign on the dotted line by the end of going through your management plan. Remember that without you as the entrepreneur or small business owner, there would be no business or no brand to speak of. What you have managed to achieve or accomplish in your life will be one of the key deciding factors for investors.

Each section in this management plan will speak to different areas of the business organization that will typically be mapped out under this part of the business plan. This section needs to be as accurate and complete as possible if you want your investors to take you and your business seriously. If you are looking at starting up with a business that only has a handful of people, then this is what needs to be included in this section under the various different headings that follow below.

Ownership Structure

Regarding ownership structure, you may be the only one running and managing the business at present; however, you might be planning on entering into a partnership agreement with the venture capitalist or the individual who funds your business (if this is necessary). Often, these individuals are happy to be silent partners. If this is the case, detail exactly what that arrangement is going to look like under this section.

For example, when coming to an agreement with angel investors or venture capitalists, they may want a majority stake in the business until such time as the business is profitable enough for you to buy them out, repaying the initial investment amount, along with any and all interest. On the other hand, some of these individuals prefer to remain in the shadows, allowing you to run the organization yourself with regular feedback sessions to ensure that the business is on track as you maneuver your way through the choppy waters of first getting into the marketplace.

Additionally, you will want to state if you are going to be the majority shareholder with one extra controlling share in the business or if the business will belong to someone else until the initial startup costs have been refunded back to those who invested in you. You may be required to relinquish that controlling share to the investors where it's only transferred back to you once your debt is settled. Be prepared for this to take a while and be realistic about how quickly your business is going to turn a profit and become successful.

While Apple turned a huge profit in their first year in business, thanks to the tenacious and brilliant sales persona that was Steve Jobs, Amazon took several years before they even broke even. Nobody can knock Jeff Bezos in the tenacious department, despite all of this. For him, just obtaining startup funding for Amazon took more than 50 business appointments, and I can assure you that not all of his financiers said "yes" to his business plan! One of the biggest lessons to be learned from both Apple and Amazons' humble garage beginnings is that anything is possible if you have a dream to make your customer's or customer's lives easier. If you chase after your passion for long enough and hard enough, you are certain to be successful (Travis, 2018; Bezos, 2020).

If you are a solo entrepreneur or small business owner without any partners, this is where you need to describe what qualifies you to be in this business and why any financier should invest in you. This is not always some fancy business degree neatly framed on a wall. More often than not, it's the sheer passion that you have for a product that will convince the powers that be that you're a worthy risk and they're then prepared to invest in your startup.

One of the most important things in this document is that you need to display a belief in yourself, your qualifications, your experience in the industry, your passion for the industry and/or the product, and the reason why they should be considering you. This document needs to convince not only them but you that you're a worthwhile investment.

If it doesn't, go back to the drawing board and continue tweaking it until it does or find another idea that ignites that flame of passion so it's burning bright enough to convince anyone to invest in you.

If you aren't passionate enough about your product, idea, concept, or service, how can you expect anyone else to back you up and support you through the initial process or the years ahead? While you may be convinced that your startup is going to be a quick success and that your product is going to fly off the shelves because people are going to be so blown away by it, well, it's good to have those dreams, but that is often not the reality. Even overnight success stories were years in the making.

Just think: If you were being asked to invest a couple of thousand dollars or maybe even millions of dollars into a startup, what is it that you would be looking for? By placing yourself in the shoes of the financier and looking at everything that you have included (or omitted) in your business plan, would you invest in your organization? This single question is probably one of the most important questions that you should be asking each step of the way when crafting your business plan.

Have you got something that people want and need? How are you personally going to drive the business to make this happen? What sets you apart from another 100 or so entrepreneurs or small business owners out there who are all competing for the same piece of the pie? Do you actually believe in yourself?

If you have other business partners, you need to repeat the above steps with each one of them. You should ask the following questions of them: What qualifies them to be an operational part of your business? What percentage of the business organization are they going to be involved with? Are they as passionate as you?

When I look back over the many startups that I've been involved with over the years, there have been many mistakes made when it came to taking on partners who hadn't been fully invested in the business with the same degree of involvement or enthusiasm, purely because they had not invested in the business financially. The school of hard knocks has a way of bringing you down a peg or two. By rights, having been schooled at the feet of a master venture capitalist (who made millions and lost just as many millions), one of the most important lessons I ever learned from him was that there will be good times (enjoy them, celebrate them, and squirrel something away during them), and when the bad times strike, you will have something to fall back on without having to give it all up and start again from scratch. The number of times you get knocked down is not important. Instead, it is the refusal to stay down and the getting right back up to face your threats or challenges directly head-on that counts.

That is the type of person you want to be, and those are the type of people you want to be in business with.

Include in this section as much about yourself and any other business partner as you can. If you graduated with an MBA from Harvard Business School, include this here. If you've had exposure to the industry by working for several market leaders, include this information here. The more information you're able to provide, the easier it is for potential investors to get to know who they are planning on backing financially.

Management Team

This section will identify the people who are part of your management team. Each of these individuals should, ideally, be experienced in the areas that you want them to operate within. There's no point in asking a logistics and distribution manager to handle human resources and administration. Similarly, if you have an IT professional in the house, there's no point handing them the reins to sales and marketing.

Your management team should be carefully selected for their skills in the area they are operating within, as well as the passion they have for the product and/or service you're looking to supply. They need to be just as excited and passionate about the business as you are or they won't be fully invested into making the business as successful as you will be.

Remember my boutique recruitment and training business from 2005? The lack of a proper business plan and the lack of passion and commitment from my partner was what led to its downfall. While I gave the business everything that I had when it came to blood and sweat equity, they weren't prepared to even meet me halfway. I worked extensive hours away from my home and my family, meeting potential candidates after hours, over weekends, and on public holidays. We offered free training to potential job seekers over weekends, and all the while, my business partner was data mining proprietary information from the business in the form of our client lists, only to be approaching them directly behind my back. It turned out she had more passion for her potential success than the success of our shared business.

You MUST ensure that you are protected from all sides against anything like this happening to you. Go into the business not trusting anyone because it will place you in a much better position as the owner of the business. If you must include individuals into your business organization and you do have specific brands, products, and trade secrets, make sure that you and your business organization are fully protected by drawing up NDAs that protect you and any information shared.

Whoever you are planning on bringing on board as part of management should be suitably qualified and experienced for the work that needs to be done. They need to be willing to take risks, especially on a business organization that's new and could potentially bomb out within the first year or so. It is worth looking for individuals who have nerves of steel.

You will notice in the appendix chapter that there is a special section for resumes, so you will add their resumes there. However, while you should provide a brief outline on who each of your management team is through their resume, this section should provide the reason for bringing them into the business in the first place. This lets potential investors understand what bonuses your team brings to the business. It will also potentially strengthen your business if they are bringing specialized skills to your business operation. In the appendix chapter, you should include your own resume and specific credentials first, followed by any and all other information as outlined in the next few sections of your business plan.

Third-Party Requirements

In previous sections, we've briefly touched on making use of specialist resources that can be outsourced on a freelance basis, and you should list all these third-party freelancers here. It is worthwhile including as much information as possible on each of your third-party suppliers so that they can be validated as reliable, quality resources. I would include these on a separate sheet where they are each listed in groups, and you are providing the business name and the name and information of the contacts you have within their business operation. Also, include contact numbers, email addresses, and a website for them to be verified. If you are already an existing client with any of these third-party vendors, it would also help adding your account details.

Many of your third-party resources would only be used briefly unless they are suppliers or manufacturers that are directly involved with your product. Third-parties you would use only for limited tasks or time frames are as follows:

1. **Event Management**

    If you're planning on working with an event management company for your initial product launch, include all the information of all parties involved. These could be a caterer, a marquee tent hire company, an event coordinator, and any other relevant individuals. If you have a master of ceremonies or a guest speaker, add them to this list as well.

2. **Design Services**

   You may need design services for your initial product branding. These third-parties could potentially be a graphic design artist, the printer, or a supplier of packaging products, such as boxes, canisters, bottles, or other unique containers. Your brand will become your single biggest asset, which makes it important to get it right from the beginning of your venture.

If your IT services can be managed offsite by a professional third-party specialist, outsource it, too. You would also include your bankers, accounts, financiers, and distributors. If you're likely to outsource your SEO and social media management to a specialist initially, include all their information here as well. Further, you want to be certain to cover things such as landlords, rental agencies, cleaning companies, and logistics or delivery companies.

Each and every third-party that's likely to become involved with your business needs to be included in this section, even if you know that you are projecting a number of years into the future and considering business growth. Be sure to still include them with an explanation of when they would be required. Even if you are uncertain of who you are going to be using to provide a specific service further down the line, forecast it so it can be included in costings and projections at a later stage. As long as it's indicated as a potential requirement, a clear indication of third-party relationships can be visible and clearly understood by anyone studying your business plan.

The following section is for those that will be involved in the day-to-day running of the business.

Human Resources

Human resources can potentially be like walking through a minefield that hasn't been cleared if you don't know what you are doing. We've already discussed signing NDAs should your product be so unique that a disgruntled employee could walk away from the business with your idea and do irreparable damage to the organization. Hopefully, your business will be employee-centered and this will never occur. Stephen R. Covey (1989/2020) makes an important point on this specific topic: "Always treat your employees exactly as you want them to treat your best customers." As a small business owner, it doesn't excuse you or exclude you from setting all the correct human resource contracts and agreements in place immediately when someone new starts with your organization.

It is worthwhile outlining your hiring process in this part of your business plan. You want to explain how you see your business expanding and the time frame for that expansion. Being able to get the timing 100% correct isn't always possible but working with a general timeline would definitely be beneficial to your business plan.

For example, my recruitment business couldn't ever predict hiring, even though we were an operation dedicated to hiring people for others! The main reason for this was we were operating our business without a functioning business plan! In our case we hired too quickly, grew at a phenomenal rate, and made a couple of poor hiring decisions (even temporary ones) that cost us dearly by the time the operation officially closed its doors in 2008/2009. One of the few things we did get right was our employment contract was airtight (which is what allowed me to rightly and legally let go of my business partner who was stealing from the business).

For your human resources model, consider the minimum number of staff you will be able to get by with as your organization gets going. If business becomes more successful, it's always easier to hire more people. This is the better way to go compared to paying employees that aren't really making any contribution toward your business or don't have enough job duties to complete because you are so new and small.

One strategy that could work well for this document is to link your hires to profit benchmarks in your business. That way, you will not only be able to afford to hire the additional people but you can really use them to help you grow your business as well.

Then, you must set out your recruitment structure. Where do you plan to find your staff? What do they look like? (Here, I am not referring to physical attributes but rather to culture.) Have you defined your corporate culture sufficiently that you can identify the type of person you'd like to have working for you? Do they need to be qualified in any particular areas?

Many companies lose out by using the type and number of degrees a person has as an essential requirement for any new hire. While there are many successful professionals out there who have loads of degrees and half the alphabet behind their names, there are just as many successful entrepreneurs with no tertiary qualifications. A great many creative entrepreneurs get bored sitting through college classes and drop out. Don't dismiss these candidates without at least meeting with them, as you might find that there's perfect synergy between you.

Did you know that Steve Jobs was one of these university dropouts who became extremely restless and needed to travel in search of "himself?" Did this make him any less effective or dynamic in what he did? The perfect synergy between him and Steve Wozniak proved to be a collaborative partnership made in heaven!

Some further shockers for you: If you're not already in the know, many of the world's wealthiest of wealthy entrepreneurs join Steve Jobs in never achieving a bachelor's degree. These include:

- Sir Richard Branson, Founder and CEO of all things Virgin
- Bill Gates of Microsoft
- Mark Zuckerberg, Founder of Facebook
- Larry Ellison, Founder of Oracle (Prince, 2014)

If you think that this is limited to Silicon Valley and it can only happen by being in the right place at the right time, then add the following individuals to the list:

- David Geffen, Co-Founder of DreamWorks, Geffen Records
- Ellen DeGeneres, Comedian and Talk Show Host
- Ted Turner, Founder of Turner Broadcasting Co. (which became CNN, the first 24-hour cable news network) (Prince, 2014)

My personal advice when considering new hires for your business would be to check each of the following boxes:

- Do they meet the requirements of the vacancy?
- Can they do the job or be taught how to do it reasonably quickly?
- Are they passionate about your business or your market sector?
- Do they fit into your company's culture? (If by this point you haven't defined what your actual company culture should look like, go back to your vision and mission statement and create a few criteria that your people would need to fall into or meet for them to fulfill your cultural fit requirement.)
- Do they look like they belong in your business?
- Do they make a good first impression?
- Are they going to make you money?
- Are they going to save you money?
- Do they have a skill that you need?

These can all be points that are included in your business plan, too.

Next, you want to define what your interview procedure looks like and list it here. For instance, state where you want to find your hires, such as through word of mouth, social media, job board websites, or even the local media. You might also want to add a plan for uploading information about open positions onto your website so that visitors know that you're hiring.

For initial hires, you may want to be handling all of this yourself. However, once your operation becomes bigger and more and more specialized, you might want to hand this over to a professional third-party hiring agency who can work to fill your vacancies confidently and professionally. This would also be something you would add to your third-party requirements section as well as here.

Hiring personnel is not as simple as glancing through a resume, being impressed with what you see, and extending an offer. It is having sufficient knowledge to ask the right questions to get to the answers you really need. It is also being able to verify the information presented in the resume document because, unfortunately, people lie. Large gaps in employment history are where some of the first important answers need to be provided. The other is reasons for leaving past jobs. If all that a candidate indicates is "personal reasons" for every single job, there's a problem and you need to dig deeper to discover what the problem stems from.

Your business plan will include your hiring process and any hiring documents that candidates will complete when applying for a job. There are loads of templates available online that you can download and modify to meet the needs of your specific business model.

Your plan should also contain a set guideline for how many candidates you'd like to interview before filling any vacancies. Ideally, this should be anywhere between three to five. If you're working through a professional agency, you can ask them to provide you with their top two or three candidates. Once you've met with the top candidates, go back through all of their details, and you might even want to draw up a strengths and weakness list for each. Don't extend any offers until you've met with them for a second time. If you have business partners, involve them in this hiring process so they remain informed and abreast of new staff members.

Indicate in this part of the plan how you plan to extend offers of employment and insert any specific documentation or clauses to be considered when hiring. If you are handling payroll and all other human resource functions within the business, it's important to be aware of the labor laws applicable to your country. Specify any stipulations or special clauses to hires in this section. If your labor laws are different for temporary or permanent hires, make a note about this here. If labor laws refer to certain statutory acts, quote those as reference numbers.

Items to be covered in the human resource section should include but not be limited to:

- disciplinary procedures
- dismissal procedures
- employment and employee contracts
- hiring processes and procedures
- job application templates
- job profile procedures
- job profile templates

In your business plan, it should suffice to mention that you have a job application template that is professional and conforms with any and all statutory requirements. It's not necessary to include all of these documents along with your business plan as this will result in it resembling a good old-fashioned telephone directory. Remember that this document should be abbreviated as much as possible while providing any interested parties as much information as they need in a concise manner. A very brief overview of all employment policies and procedures according to statutory or business requirements could be mentioned, but due to how extensive and specific these documents are, it's not necessary to attach them. It's enough that each of these documents is listed without providing physical evidence at this stage.

Take it from someone who has been there: Making sure that you have all of this information in place is crucial to the overall success of your business. While you are working on getting your business up and running, spend some time putting this mountain of paperwork together (and it is literally a mountain of paperwork). If you are not clued up on HR, outsource it and hand it over to a professional to manage it for you. There are plenty of individuals in the freelance directories who could put all of these things together for you, while you focus your efforts and attention on those things that need to be prioritized right now. If this is the route that's more effective for you, then add this resource to your third-party list above.

Chapter 7: Operating Plan

"Remember to celebrate milestones as you prepare for the road ahead."

~ Nelson Mandela, South African Leader

The operating plan included in your overall business plan is going to get down to the cogs that keep the engine of the business turning in any one particular direction. This is where all the dreaming actually becomes a reality. It's where you get down, dirty, and roll your sleeves up to get the work done that needs doing.

Operating plans are often referred to as strategic plans, because it is vital for any business to know which direction they're actually moving in. While all the other plans to this point have been focused on what could be, your operating plan should be focused on what actually is happening or what needs to be happening to reach your goals.

An operating plan tells you what needs to be done, who is responsible for doing it, when it needs to be done, and which department of the business the task falls under. Your strategic plan should incorporate your business or departmental goals, who is responsible for actioning each goal, the outcome that you hope to achieve, and the reporting structure.

Strategic Planning

To help you understand the ins and outs of a strategic plan, it's best to work with a real example. So, here, we will go over an operational plan for starting a warehousing and distribution business for branded promotional items.

On paper, a strategic plan would look something like this:

<u>Goal 1</u>: Obtain combination office and warehouse space to accommodate goods as well as staff. A minimum of 500 square feet of warehousing space is necessary with 10-12 offices, ablution facilities, easy access for loading and unloading of vehicles, sufficient parking for five delivery vehicles, off-road access, and a professional reception area.

<u>Responsible party</u>: Business owner, warehousing, logistics, operations, and administration managers.

<u>Department(s)</u>: Executive management team.

Date Due: November 30, 2020

Goal 2: Identify list of promotional items to be branded for resale to larger corporates. A complete list of a minimum of 100-200 different promotional items are to be identified with samples sourced to check each item for quality and branding purposes. Confirmation of line items to be stocked and resold to larger customers, such as the automotive industry, restaurant franchises, hotels, or any organization that has a need for branded promotional items on a regular basis.

Responsible party: Marketing manager, sales manager and/or sales representatives, and warehouse manager (to be consulted regarding space requirements).

Department: Sales, marketing, and warehouse departments.

Date Due: October 31, 2020

Goal 3: Increase sales revenue for XYZ brand over Q3 and Q4 (the third and fourth quarters of the financial year).

Responsible party: Sales and marketing managers and sales personnel, including key accounts managers.

Department: Sales and marketing.

Due Date: December 2020

And so you would continue down with a list of additional strategic goals and objectives that need to be achieved within the business. This could form part of a table where goals are fleshed out to become actionable items and those responsible for completing each task can clearly see what they're responsible for along with due dates to meet a specific timeline.

One of the key criteria when it comes to this section of the business plan is that you can provide the reader with a clear blueprint of what you've already done in your business so far, and what you plan to do in the future to increase market share, brand visibility, sales turnover, and more. This is where you need to pull out all the stops to present potential investors with a clear idea of how far you've already come, and how far you could potentially go in the future with their help.

There are a number of key headings and items to be taken into consideration when it comes to operations, but these are all physical things. They are tangible and can be easily understood. When compiling your operational plan, you need to be realistic when it comes to what is involved in the day-to-day running of your business.

Production

Whether or not you are physically manufacturing anything, you probably have a product or service that needs to be managed effectively daily, and this should be a part of your operating plan. Even if you have a third-party production facility, similar to my sporting goods experience, you need to understand their business as well as you understand your own.

When I first teamed up with this operation, I knew absolutely nothing about the product and/or any of the components that would be used in the manufacturing process. I was warned that it was going to be a baptism by fire and I would need to either sink or swim. But swim I did! With the occasional help of a life raft!

I made it my business to get to know every single minute item that went into making the product. I would often spend days with our manufacturer going over flaws and where the product needed to be strengthened and reinforced until it was 100% perfect. Even then, we would hold regular progress meetings in the factory where I was able to inspect the goods directly as they were coming off the production line.

There were strong bonds formed between ourselves and our manufacturing team. There had to be mutual trust and respect, so when I needed to place a rush order, I could rest easy knowing that it would be taken care of. You need to make your third-party vendor an extension of your business (or at least think of them that way). They will be loyal to you and work extra shifts or overtime to make certain you receive your products on time, even when you're placing just-in-time (JIT) orders.

If you have more than one manufacturer, stipulate all the information about them that may be required for any financier to make an informed decision regarding your business based on the facts rather than some of the nice-to-haves that may have been included in some of the other areas of your business plan. Provide the reasons why you are working with the manufacturers that you are. This could be anything from convenience, location, price, quality, or skill. Or, it could be as simple as they're the only supplier that's able to produce the product according to the specifications and the quality that you need at the right price. Also include every single component that goes into manufacturing your product from initial design to final packaging.

Consider the following example as a business model for the production part of your operational plan:

You've decided to start a boutique-style vintage candy distribution company. You can work from home at the moment as you have a wholesale supplier for the candy. Your goals, at present, are having some absolutely fabulous vintage labels designed and printed, repackaging the items, taking orders online, ensuring payment is received, shipping, and following through. Simple enough? Maybe. You invested $5,000 in candy and in a good quality printer that can print professional labels. Your investment has allowed you to keep a certain amount of stock of your fast-moving items and collect from your manufacturer for any special orders.

So, your production process flow will look something like this:

1. You receive an order for five dozen boxes of cranberry nougat.
2. You confirm the order with your online client and provide them with an automated invoice along with your company banking details.
3. You currently have enough cranberry nougat for 10 dozen boxes.
4. You have all of your vintage packaging labels already designed, ready to be printed and stuck on vintage recycled packaging. You print out the five dozen labels that you need, label each of the boxes, and package the nougat as well as reinforcing it into a larger box for shipping along with the customer details.
5. Once all of this has taken place, you make contact with your delivery channel (courier service/door-to-door delivery/curbside pickup/counter-to-counter delivery) that your customer has selected. From the moment the package is handed over to your delivery channel, they take over your communication with your client. This could be an area that could be potentially weak in your operational plan that may need to be tweaked at a later stage or you could still confirm with your customer that their order is on its way.

There are still a couple of steps that need to be processed as part of this business. The first is that you've now used up half of your cranberry nougat on one order. This needs to be replaced to keep your stock levels accurate and up-to-date. In addition to the stock that you need to replenish, you have used five dozen boxes, five dozen labels, and a percentage of inks from your printer. Each of these things should have been included in the costing of your product as well as in your profit margin.

Certain other costs are incurred, which you may not have considered as actual costs. These are:

- your home that you're currently working out of
- your motor vehicle that you're collecting various raw materials with (such as boxes, labels, stock from the candy manufacturer, and ink cartridges for your printer)
- your mobile device that you're making contact with the client on
- your laptop, iPhone, and iPad that you're currently using for your online business
- any additional costs, such as data, website hosting, advertising costs, and more

In your business plan, each of these things should be clearly mentioned and form part of your costing scenario and operating plan; otherwise, you will be losing money hand over fist forever. While your initial $5,000 investment in candy and the printer may have provided you with a small cushion, it's most certainly not likely to make you a fortune overnight unless you've positioned your product in the right place in the market to be charging a premium price.

Something that hasn't been discussed in this section of your business plan, which should be included along with your process flow under production or manufacturing, would be potential risks.

Risks

Every business faces risks, whether they want to admit it or not. Your business plan should include every single risk you can think of, no matter how small or insignificant you think it might be. Risks could be anything, which makes this part of the business plan a little difficult to put together. To help get on the right track, below are some examples of risks.

One risk could be incorrectly predicting the amount of stock you need. In other words, running out of stock when you have a lead time to replace it or shrinkage (onsite product theft usually perpetrated by staff.)

Other risks could include what are referred to as "acts of God." This would be fire, flood, or hail damage, which are not always covered by insurance.

Another risk could be a break-in. This happened to one of my clients I was consulting. A break-in cost them their computers and televisions that were used for marketing purposes in their reception area. Within a 10-minute window, their offices were breached and every office was tossed. There was no trace of the culprits, yet the damage they left in their wake hit the company hard. All their accounting and financial information was lost, their design information was lost, customer databases were gone, and many of their organization's trade secrets were on the computers that were stolen from various divisions within the company.

Risks need to be mitigated as best as you can, and having mentioned insurance above, it is one of the ways to protect yourself. When taking insurance, try and arrange for an all-risks coverage, even if it may cost you a little extra each month. You never know when a pipe may burst, flooding offices and/or destroying expensive office equipment that is necessary for you to continue operating. More importantly, insurance can cover you if there's a break-in and you happen to lose proprietary information that's on computers or laptops, such as client lists, banking information, or other important documentation that you've invested a substantial amount of money in.

Even though they had insurance, my client couldn't put a price on the information that they had gathered over years and years of being in business. It's easy to ensure you're sufficiently covered for physical losses but make certain that your insurance allows data recovery, too. It's wise to revise your insurance coverage every 6 to 12 months as your business is growing.

Another recommendation is that when you are working with proprietary information, you want to ensure you backup to either the cloud or to an external source to secure your intellectual property, making the transition back a lot smoother. Do this, even if it means backing up at the end of every day. It's far less costly than losing the information that you may have spent years acquiring or building up.

In your business plan, include a section that is going to indicate exactly how you plan to minimize and deal with any and all risks that could potentially harm your business. As an example, let's take a look at a promotional item business. Their risks would include accidents where a vehicle is damaged so severely that it needs to be scrapped, items being damaged in transit, items not printed correctly, delivery issues, clients not paying for items, and theft.

You need to have plans in place for every possible scenario that might go wrong. This is not to say that it's going to go wrong. Instead, it's a way for you to consider all the variables in front of you in a realistic manner. When considering your risk and what to put in your business plan, consider the things that hold a lot of value for you. For example, a motor vehicle or specialized software that performs specific functions. Some design software programs can cost thousands of dollars and to lose these, along with designs, could be devastating to your business. You want to ensure that you are including every single aspect of the day-to-day operations of your business within this section about potential risks.

Facilities

In this part of the business plan, you need to either provide detailed information about what type of facilities you need and why you need them or provide information about the facilities that you've managed to already secure. There are a couple of pointers here that are vitally important. The first is "location, location, location!"

Let's return to our vintage candy business model from earlier. You may have been working from home until now, but your business is ready to take the next step by finding suitable premises.

You are currently facing a number of questions that you need to be able to answer. Do you continue operating purely as an online service where you hire a smallish warehouse that has a couple of staff picking and packing the candy, forming a better production chain? Or, do you go all in and take a two-pronged approach to the market where you decide to distribute directly as well as online? How is this going to affect your business model moving forward?

First off, your $5,000 candy stock holding is not going to work. You will probably need to invest in a much bigger range than what you're offering online, as you will need to fill an entire storefront. So far, you may have advertised multiple products online using creative photography and capturing the vintage image of your brand. To recreate this same image in an actual store is going to take finding exactly the right facility.

If you're opting for the vintage look, then what you should ideally be looking for should be a strip mall that has either a completely neutral look that could be turned into a storefront that looks like a vintage candy store or a location that's standalone and is already close to being authentically vintage.

By finding a freestanding old cottage-style home, you may need to jump through a couple of hoops if you need business zoning rights to trade from the property. This is the type of information you're going to need to investigate and provide full disclosure for here. You may find that renting a home as a storefront could be a cheaper option than opening a store in a strip mall.

However, the strip mall may receive way more passing foot traffic than what a home tucked away in suburbia will. You may need to weigh all the pros and cons for each before finally deciding.

Whichever route you take, it's going to require a much larger investment than keeping minimal stock in a controlled environment in your home while trading only online. One of the main questions to ask yourself would be how far you'd like to go when it comes to growing your business. Do you want to remain in control of the business or are you happy to hand over the reins to someone else?

These are all things that you need to include in your business plan along with the timelines that you foresee this growth taking place. This growth is predictive, and because of this, it's not always 100% accurate. You never know what the future is likely to bring.

Try and set various milestones as indicative markers of growth rather than an actual timeline. It may be easier to predict that by the time your business reaches x amount of product each month for three to six months, it's time to take things up a notch! Find wise ways to reinvent your business and propose business growth on paper where investors can actually recognize that once you are turning over amounts as specified, you will need to consider expansion in terms of facilities.

Staffing

In the last chapter, we spoke extensively about the human resources element which included the how of adding new people into your organization or business. In this section, it's important to understand the what and the why as well as the when. Much of the purpose of this book so far has been to prompt you to discover why you feel the need to accomplish certain things or what is going to drive and motivate you to expand current operations. Well, now it's time to use that drive and motivation in making important staffing decisions.

This part of your business plan is going to specify each of the positions that you need to fill within your organization as it grows. While the previous chapter also covered how you are going to bring these people on board and where you plan on finding them, this section (because it is the nuts and bolts of your business plan) is going to include exactly which positions you need to fill and the type of individuals needed to fill them. You should try to provide a timeline of when you want these positions filled as well. Similar to business growth, this is not always possible to predict accurately. Benchmarks may be the only accurate prediction for hiring the staff you need, so try to include those.

As a regular startup business, you may not have a choice but to hire under-qualified staff in key positions when you really need them to be there. For my recruitment and training business, there was a receptionist and a personal assistant along with my partner and myself. Initially, the business felt having to carry the weight of the two additional workers; however, they were a very necessary addition to the business if we planned to grow.

My personal assistant did everything from pre-screening candidates to typing CVs for me to check before delivering them to clients. Although I had to take a hands-on training role with her, she was a pivotal part of my business, and without her, my partner and I would not have had the freedom to work on what really mattered within the business: securing new clients and concentrating on finding candidates. This is the type of information about staffing that you should include in your plan.

In this section of the business plan, identify the type of individuals you are going to need to grow your business and when. For instance, I would explain the role of the personal assistant, why they were needed, and when I needed someone to fill that role (right away, it turned out). Finding individuals who are hungry to learn and grow has always been one of my key criteria when I've hired staff within any organization that I've owned.

It may be worthwhile for you to complete a job master template for all key personnel that you believe would be necessary within your business organization. These need to be as detailed as possible so that you have the basics to work with. Once you know and understand what you need, finding the who is a lot easier.

Have you ever sat in an interview or business meeting with someone and there seems to be an immediate connection? This is, ideally, what you're looking for with any of the individuals you're planning to hire. There needs to be a close bond between you and those you work with. It needs to become a collaborative effort.

Detail each individual that will be needed in the business organization and by when. While you may currently be outsourcing much of your work at present, there comes a time when you are going to need to bring these positions in-house. Once your workload and workflow have picked up sufficiently, you will know when the time is right to consider hiring these individuals on a permanent basis. Specify this on a timeline so investors can see how you're planning on gearing up your business.

Equipment

Your operating plan should also include the equipment you need for your business. For many entrepreneurs or small business owners, your plan might only include a laptop or desktop computer, a printer, data that's reliable and always on, a tablet, and a smartphone. However, you would also want to account for the equipment your business will need as it changes over time.

For example, let's turn back to our vintage candy store example. As you grow beyond just operating out of your own home and move into a larger facility or storefront, you will need to invest in specific point-of-sale (POS) cash registers and all your products would need to carry a barcode or ScanSnap marker so that they could be identified when scanned during a sale. You may also need an accurately calibrated weight measurement system that will allow your customers to mix their candies and only pay by the weight. Point of sale shelving and other vintage décor will be needed to create the correct ambience within the business, including lighting, counters, props, or display pieces. Further, you may need refrigerators for certain items or for an extended product range of vintage drinks that you've managed to source and collaborate with another supplier on.

You'll notice that nothing is quite as cut and dry as it seems at first. You may think that it's simple to open a brand-new business; however, without getting every single aspect right from the start, your business that was doing extremely well online could prove to be a direct selling bust!

Before you open your business, and while you're populating your business plan, keep asking these questions: "Is there more?" and "What else?" This will allow you to recognize whether you have everything that you need listed or if you can take things a step further and imagine what you might need in the future.

You also want to think about how you will fund all the additional equipment. To figure this out, place each piece of equipment that you need on a list of line items with several different prices for each. My recommendation would be to work from a three-quote system, meaning that you always have three price quotes to consider for each piece of equipment. This doesn't always mean that you need to accept the first quote issued or the cheapest quote that's out there, but it will help you compare apples to apples so that you can make an informed decision about the equipment you need and how it fits into your overall budget. By creating a list like this in your business plan, you will give yourself and your investors a good idea of the assets you have now and what assets you will need in the future.

Supplies

Along with equipment, you also want to state what supplies you have and will need as well as who your suppliers are (suppliers could be anyone from printing companies that design your logo and your business cards to the actual suppliers of raw material to be used in your product). If you're offering a service of some description, your supplies and suppliers may look a little different than a business offering a product. For example, you may be paying a freelance supplier for SEO services to advertise your services on the right platforms or may have a supplier where you get your promotional items from.

Further, if you are only involved in the service industry, such as business consulting or training, it becomes slightly more difficult to identify what your supplies are unless you're running workshops that provide each delegate with extensive notes for them to work through during your seminars. In this instance, you would need paper, a method of binding workbooks, handouts, and other materials. You may also need to provide stationery of some description to your students as well as a certificate of course completion.

If you recall the business of branded promotional items example we used in the strategic planning section, the list of supplies for that business may look something like this:

- line items (100 to 200) with sufficient stock levels to rotate orders, branding them quickly
- bins and a proper warehousing racking system where stock can be stored efficiently for easy access
- office supplies, such as paper, folders, pens, paper clips, and so on
- food and drinks for the breakroom
- brochures for sales and marketing purposes
- professional photographs of line items for the website
- promotional materials, such as business cards, banners, car wraps, flyers, and so on

As you work through this section of your business plan, keep asking yourself: "Is there more?" and "Am I forgetting anything?" If you are, add these to the list.

Include the terms and prices that each of your suppliers are prepared to give you should you pursue working with them. This could be one way of keeping initial startup costs down. You don't always need to go with the most expensive option when you first start out. When we started our recruitment and training business in 2005, we purchased the bare minimum we needed in office furniture from a second-hand dealer. This gave us the chance of seeing whether our business was likely to succeed or not in the first 6 to 12 months without wasting a lot of money on supplies that we wouldn't need if we didn't succeed. Fortunately, the business was extremely successful and we were able to buy brand-new office furniture once we moved into larger premises at the end of our first year.

If you are a startup, consider everything that you will need for your first 12 to 24 months in business and write this down in your business plan. While this may boggle your mind for a while and you will probably forget some really important items, include a buffer into your financial plan (which is where all the costs of these items will go) that will allow you some wiggle room, especially when it comes to identifying supplies. If you're moving into offices and/or warehousing facilities, one of the best ways to work with this list is to physically work through each room at a time according to the floorplan of the business. This way, it's slightly more difficult to forget about key items necessary for individuals to perform their tasks to the very best of their abilities.

Industry Affiliation

If you are or want to become a member of a professional organization in your specific industry, then you want to list them here. For some businesses, belonging to a professional group or association could be a real game changer. An example of this would be an accounting business belonging to the American Institute of CPAs (ACIPA). These types of memberships validate your business and give you credibility, as you have shown that you have met membership criteria and are serious about your field. It lets prospective clients know that they are working with a professional institution and their business dealings with you will be on the up and up.

If you have a registration certificate or certification from them, it may help placing this on your wall in a classy frame or confirm this validation on your website so those dealing with you are aware of what associations you are a member of.

Maybe you're only planning on joining a specific association because you're a startup, but you still want to indicate this on your business plan so that your potential investors have a better idea of what you're planning to achieve and that you have a goal to move in the right direction. The one thing with regards to governing institutions is that there are always high-quality standards and conditions that they use as a benchmark. If your potential investors can see that it's your intention to aim high and achieve these standards, whether they're local, national, or international, they will see that you are serious about running a professional and ethical business.

Quality Control

As part of your operating plan, you must indicate what quality control measures you are putting in place. All industries need a degree of quality control, whether you're operating as a small business enterprise or even as a solo entrepreneur. Quality control comes in many forms and should be designed around your business models and needs.

In the sporting goods environment, apart from the third-party manufacturer and all of their own in-house quality checks, we would perform random checks on the product ourselves as well as stopping over at the factory to do spot checks on their production line. This company was already accredited with ISO 9000 certification (which is an international standard that includes quality management and assurance), but we still needed to confirm that our brand was protected. These control measures were in place from the very beginning, so it was not unusual for us to arrive and complete an unannounced inspection.

So, in our business plan, we were sure to include all of the processes for safety control and included a section on how our manufacturer was conducting quality control and how we did so ourselves as well.

As another example, let's once again return to our vintage candy company. Quality control for this type of business might mean that you have to be in regular touch with your supplier about what their safety and quality standards are and ask for regular reports about their testing measures. This information would be vital to include in your business plan. You might even want to hire a company that could do quality control on your packaging. For example, testing how different packing materials react to heat, how well they protect the candy product under certain extreme conditions (as you ship a lot of candy), or if the packaging includes any harmful substances that could affect the candy. You might even taste test the quality of your candy, too, which will be one very good perk!

As you can see, you want your quality control plan to take into account a number of different factors, and this section will depend on the type of business you are. For instance, a consulting business like mine might include information about running quality checks on the materials used for training sessions (and it wouldn't need to be a very in-depth section). If you are planning on selling something, however, your potential investors want to know what steps you have and will take to ensure the quality of your product.

Special Needs

The last section of your operating plan needs to specify any special needs that you may have in your business operations. For example, a special need might include needing to remain compliant with labor laws or safety standards within your manufacturing or production environment.

In order to do that, you might need to lay out in your operating plan that all staff will receive or have received basic health and safety training, and that you have an ongoing plan for keeping their training up-to-date to remain compliant with local, state, or federal laws and regulations. It would be your responsibility as the owner of the business to ensure that this happens. If you are unsure of these standards yourself, it's best to call on the services of a suitably qualified professional to handle this health and safety training as and when required.

Other specific needs could include excessive amounts of water and/or electricity supply to your manufacturing facility. You may need more people because tasks cannot be automated further. You may need to be located close to an airport or train station because your core business is vehicle hire or closely related to tourism.

Whatever your specific special needs are, include them right here. There should be no surprises once you start your business because you have already taken the time to fully map out your strategic and operational plan for every part and piece of your business. Everything that you are planning on doing or are currently doing, should be detailed in the operating plan section as a part of your complete business plan.

Chapter 8: Financial Plan

"Our goals can only be reached through a vehicle of a plan in which we must fervently believe, and upon which we must vigorously act. There is no other route to success."

~ Pablo Picasso

While this is the final part of the actual business plan document, it deserves to be carefully prepared, and all the information contained in this section of the plan should be 100% accurate and correct (unlike previous parts that allow for some projecting and forecasting on your part). Once you and your investors are done crunching all the numbers, your financial plan will confirm three very important things. First, it will confirm whether or not your product or service is going to make money. Second, it will confirm how much money it is or isn't going to make. Third, it will confirm whether you actually have an idea or a product that's worth pursuing or not.

After thoroughly going over your financial plan, potential investors will know whether or not they want to go into business with you. That's why this part of your business plan is so important. All the other sections may show your competence, drive, passion, and ability to plan and run a business, but this section will tell you and your investors whether your business makes financial sense to pursue.

Although the financial plan only boils down to four specific things, these will give any potential investors a crystal clear view of your entire business. This is one of the reasons why it's important for you to be as accurate and honest as possible with all the numbers and information you provide here. This is also where investors will see what you've been able to do with your business to date and what room there is to expand and grow the business further. The information provided to them in each of the sections below will determine whether or not they're prepared to invest and take a chance on both your business idea and you.

If your business has already been in operation for any particular length of time, you will be able to provide potential investors with genuine numbers. If you're still only in your startup phase as an entrepreneur, you can still provide this information; however, your first year on your income statement is likely to look pretty dismal. One of the main reasons for this is that you are going to be sitting with a lot of zero figures on these documents unless you're already investing some of the working capital yourself.

Investors who are looking at a startup want to see what their initial investment is going to come to, and they then need to know how much it's going to continue to cost for the initial period of the business before it becomes profitable and viable to them. That is, once the business shows sufficient profit for them to be able to withdraw part of their investment or to see a return on investment, also known as ROI, which is all to say that you must still provide financial information even if you're only a startup.

There are some extremely important things that need to be completed at the time of opening any business. Whether you've been trading as a solo entrepreneur and your business is ready for its next step or you're looking for startup capital, you must complete the below steps and adhere to the following rules and regulations:

1. Your business needs to be officially registered in order for you to operate legally. Make certain that you complete any and all statutory or regulatory requirements so that you don't face hefty fines or penalties later.
2. You must register for tax purposes. Once you have received your business registration documents, use this information to register your business for tax and any other statutory payments that may be necessary in your country or state of operation.
3. You may even need to register your business with a trade union or affiliate organization. If this is so, do it at this stage and include all the costs in the income and expenditure section below.

Your financial plan will provide investors with all of the following information as well:

1. **Details of Your Bank Account(s)**

    You need to include information about your financial institutions, such as their address and all of your account details. This would include account numbers and SWIFT codes if imports or exports are part of your business. It's vitally important that you keep your personal banking account separate from your business banking account. That way, should anything happen with the business, it's not going to affect your personal financial standing with your bank. Additionally, you will need to find a reputable bank that possibly invests in entrepreneurs or small business startups.

2. **Your Accountant's Information**

    You must also include information about who your accountant is because this is the person who will be responsible for ensuring that your financial records are accurate. While you could have an accountant as a permanent part of your business staff later on down the road, it's important that an independent and impartial accountant is able to go over your financial records on a regular basis for tax purposes and regular, accurate reporting. Larger organizations that have been trading for some time are used to providing financial statements on an annual basis, and smaller organizations and startups should look at providing these reports more regularly to investors as well. This will allow them to see that you are serious about the business and also where their money has gone or is going.

Income Statements

The first part of your financial plan will be your income statements, which need to list every line item that you're proposing to sell or service you're looking to provide against a historical track record. Your income statements need to have all forms of income, losses, and expenses over the given time frame. An income statement would also need to include a section where there are projections for the future.

For a business to be profitable and viable to any investor, this income statement should, ideally, show an upward curve in your business and sales that can be verified, recorded, and accurately broken down if it were mapped out using a bar graph. Month by month or year by year, there should be an upward trend for the company to appear attractive to investors. Once again, if you've been operating for a while, you will be able to provide accurate data indicating business growth that can be seen from official bank records or provided by your accountant.

One of the reasons your income statement should be broken down to line items individually is so that you can clearly see at the end of each month, quarter, or financial year whether a product or service is performing or not. If something is not working, you can include in your business plan potential solutions for turning the product around or you can include a plan to cut the product altogether.

If something is no longer profitable, especially on paper, you would begin to see a downward trend taking place on your income statement. Think of it this way: You have roughly 50 line items on your income statement and there are five that seem to be draining funds from the business rather than making it money. Any way you slice it, you have two options facing you: You can cut your losses with the five line items and replace them with something that could potentially make you more money or you can simply discontinue them altogether (leaving you with only 45 line items). For most entrepreneurs, they would probably choose the first route and look for alternative ways to make money.

Either way, including this information along with your income statements shows you have a well-thought strategy.

You don't want to provide or predict false or wrong numbers on this document. As much of it is guesswork, you should ultimately provide three sets of figures on this document: a column that represents the worst-case scenario, a second that represents average growth, and a third that represents the best possible outcome.

One of the main reasons for this is that you need to show your potential investors that you're not living in a world of make-believe, and you've removed any rose-tinted glasses that may have made you think that you're going to enter the market and everything is going to be 100% all profits and sunshine from the outset. You are going to face challenging months, and there will be times when your product doesn't perform as well as you'd like it to. Remember that you have no way whatsoever of being able to predict the outcome of the business in the future. There could be factors completely out of your control that might negatively affect and influence your product and your business, and this is why you need to be realistic rather than aggressive with the numbers.

To get to the point of being able to determine whether or not your business is going to provide a profit or loss, you can look at the following formula:

Income – Expenditure = Profit or Loss

Every conceivable outcome of this equation should be shown on this document to prove to potential investors that you have done your homework and you're providing them with the most accurate data possible. The income statement is where you can see the profit and loss (P & L) of a business as it shows both income and expenditure. Your income statement should include a discussion or list of income and expenditures.

Income means monies coming into the business, either through investments from financiers or where you've invested the money yourself. Income could also come from actual sales of your product if you've already been operating.

Expenditure is everything that you've got to pay for from raw materials that go into manufacturing your product at every single stage to getting it ready to go to market. Expenditure is usually divided into two separate categories known as fixed expenditure and variable expenditure. A fixed expenditure is a cost that isn't likely to change and is usually the same each and every month, while a variable expenditure is one that is dependent on other factors and can be different month by month. Let's look at breaking these two down even further.

Fixed Expenditure

A fixed expenditure could include things like your office rental or lease costs, which stay the same each month. If you're paying for certain utility services, such as internet, data, telephone, or cable, then these costs will remain the same every month as well. If you currently have a third-party freelancer that you're keeping on with some form of retainer each month or a staff that is on a regular salary, this expenditure should be included here. If you're operating from a large warehousing facility, there's bound to be some costs that will remain stagnant each month. Basically, any cost that doesn't change would be included here.

In this section, it may be worthwhile completing a separate column and providing the calculations that are just for your initial startup costs. Your initial startup costs are always much higher than what your normal monthly fixed expenditure costs would be as you must pay deposits and other expenses. This will help you keep track of one-off startup payments that need to be made as well as providing investors with a clear enough picture of what they're in for.

Variable Expenditure

Variable monthly costs are those that can fluctuate from month to month and aren't always the same. Depending on the type of business you are, you might have a lot of variable expenditures or very little. For example, if you're a manufacturing business, then your expenditures would depend on what your sales have been or how many orders have been received, which would then dictate how much you spend on raw materials.

Likewise, if you're a business that must keep a minimum stock of products as a buffer, then as this stock moves out, you need to keep replacing and replenishing your stock so that your minimum level remains constant. But the amount you spend on replacing and replenishing would vary each month, depending on how much you sold or didn't sell.

Other things that are variable expenditures are things like stationery costs, fuel costs, sales and marketing costs, and even business credit card bills. If your sales team is submitting expenses for entertaining clients at lunches or meeting up with clients in coffee shops, these expenses aren't going to be the same monthly, either.

Within your business plan, your section on your income statements will include all the information about your fixed and variable expenditures. This will give your investors a clear picture of where you are spending money and how much you are spending. Ideally, your expenditures should not be more than your income as this shows that you aren't actually making money. If this is the case, then you would want to see where you can reduce your expenditures so that your financial plan looks better.

Balance Sheet

A business balance sheet is usually only generated at the end of each financial year that an organization has been in business. You can agree with your financial accountant when your financial year end is going to be. Most organizations operate between March and the end of February the following year or from the middle of the year to the middle of the following year. Other organizations choose to operate from the time that they are open for a full year (choosing these periods to be their financial year). Whichever route you have agreed to take with your financial advisor or your accountant, this section is where you would stipulate this information.

Your balance sheet only focuses on the following three areas each year:

1. Assets
2. Liabilities
3. Equity

Assets

There are several different types of business assets that could show up on your balance sheet. First, there are fixed assets, which are those things that might include buildings, factories, or warehouses that you own and don't rent. They can also include anything that you don't owe any money on like purchases that you made as part of your startup costs. This could be large appliances like office refrigerators, microwaves, televisions, computers, printers, and more. Although these are fixed assets, they depreciate over time, and so the longer you have them, the more they will continue to lose value.

There are also variable assets that are things like your inventory, which changes all the time as you sell more products, and any accounts receivable where you are owed money but the amount varies at times. If you're sitting with a lot of bad debt, this will be reflected here, but it will also indicate that you need to be able to do something to fix what you're currently doing to ensure that this doesn't happen too often.

You should be keeping an asset register as part of your bookkeeping function. This is recommended rather than leaving it until you're about to issue a financial report at the end of your fiscal year or put together this part of your business plan.

Liabilities

Liabilities are what you owe to other people. This could be anything from lease agreements for motor vehicles or other equipment to your monthly expenses, such as utility bills. If you've been keeping up-to-date with all of these expenses each month, then your assets should outweigh your liabilities once your startup costs have been repaid to any investors. Up until the time that your assets have been repaid, they will always form part of this section of your balance sheet.

Equity (Value)

Equity is the overall value that's in your business. It's what's left once you've deducted your liabilities from your assets. Just as we had a previous equation to work out whether your business is worthwhile, your balance sheet is going to be able to provide you and your investors with similar information when you combine each of these three components:

Equity = Assets – Liabilities

Your balance sheet, which is included in your financial plan, needs to summarize each of the three components briefly. It should not be a rambling explanation under each heading but rather should be a few sentences to provide some background information. Try to just highlight the most important points under each heading that either shareholders or investors need to be made aware of. When you're generating your financial plan, the best way to complete this section is to generate a proforma invoice. As mentioned earlier, your first year's figures are going to look rather dismal, and a proforma invoice will show correct forecasts for your future equity, assets, and liabilities.

Cash Flow Projections for First Several Years

The second part of your financial plan is the cash flow projections section. This document is very important as it's going to highlight times when you may need financial assistance in order for your business to survive. Remember, I mentioned that some businesses are seasonal. It's this type of environment where you're facing those off-seasons that your business may battle for a while until you establish your brand in the marketplace sufficiently well for you to manage these seasons without financial assistance.

So, what do I mean by cash flow projections? As the words indicate, you're going to try and predict how money is going to flow in and out of your business over a specific period of time. In this instance, as a startup, you should manage your predictions for the first couple of years or as far as you think that you can. Here, you're going to look at things like your initial startup costs and how long it's going to take to get your business up and running, especially if you're manufacturing.

With the sporting goods product I worked on, before we sold one unit or went to launch, it was months and months of preparation, planning, working with samples, and searching for the right manufacturers for the various components we needed. Hence, the venture capitalist that funded the entire operation was already a couple of million down before we ever even moved into production. But he knew that the product would be a winner in the right markets and also knew what needed to be done and when, all because we had done our homework.

For the sporting goods product, our cash flow projection took into account the amount of money that went into each of the steps of creating the product (this would be our downtime when we need the most financial help). For example, we budgeted for designs, sample materials, and the many components. Although we knew that all this money would be going out, we knew that in the backend we would make it up. So, our cash flow analysis also took into account the numbers we had for potential sales that were based on a similar product already in the market. This is just a small example of what this type of document might look like.

For you, if you're only a startup, you've already done the work of figuring out what you need for your business in terms of supplies, facilities, production, staff, and more (remember your operating plan?). You can now use that information as a part of your cash flow document and project into the future what your possible costs and profits will be.

There are certain things that any business needs to get up off the ground. You need your business registration and other statutory documents, which you need to pay for. You may want to get your website and online marketing presence up and running while you're busy sorting out business premises and other startup items. Once again, this is going to require an investment, not only in the design of the site, but you may need someone to blog and interact with your customers and/or potential customers for you. This is the type of information a cash flow projection would include.

Essentially, this is the part of your business plan where you provide your wish list of all the things you want and need to make your business work from the get-go. Sometimes, it's a great idea to indicate these by splitting these into the two separate columns: wants and needs. Other columns should be broken down into different required items according to the timeline.

Investors want to be able to see how long it's going to take before your business can start seeing cash flowing back into your bank account. They need to decide whether it's going to be a matter of months or a matter of years before they will begin to see a return on their investment.

The cash flow analysis document will also show them whether or not you can be trusted with their money. Someone who is realistic and thorough about these projections is clearly someone who knows what they are doing. Most investors also want to know what you're prepared to put into the business yourself.

It's important that you don't provide them with a cash flow statement rather than a cash flow projection. The difference between the two is that the cash flow statement has already happened in the past (statement), while the cash flow projection is a prediction of what might happen in the future. I've mentioned on several occasions that we have no idea what the future has in store for us, but this document should make the best predictions it can based on real numbers and data.

Your cash flow projection should be for at least a 12-month period that is broken down into each month. This is for exact planning purposes and so investors can see what type and total of investment they should be considering. This timeline gives them a good sense as to whether your business is creditworthy and whether you are worth taking the financial risk on as an individual. It will allow them to determine whether your line of credit needs to be short-, medium-, or long-term and also approximately how much credit you will need. All of this information will provide them with a better understanding of how you see your business playing out in your own mind over the 12-month period from the time of their investment.

To get down to nuts and bolts, a cash flow projection statement consists of three separate parts:

1. Cash Income
2. Cash Outflow
3. Balance of Income to Outflow

Cash Income

This is your estimated cash month-to-month income projections for the first year of business operations. The only information you're capturing here is monies being received as a direct result of the sales of your goods or services.

Cash Outflow

Working from your ledger (where you've listed all your expenditure items), copy each line item that is a monthly expense. You can group each of these items so you don't forget anything. For example:

- Rentals
- Offices
- Furniture
- Equipment
- Vehicles
- Vehicle Maintenance
- Logistics
- Fuel
- Courier Services
- Postage Costs
- Shipping
- Forwarding and Clearing
- Manufacturing
- Manufacturing Costs
- Raw Materials
- Item A
- Item B
- Item C
- Sales and Marketing
- Printing and Packaging
- Public Relations
- Advertising
- Point of Sale
- Marketing Material
- Sales Merchandising
- Social Media Marketing

- SEO
- Website
- IT Services
- IT Retainer
- IT Maintenance
- Equipment
- Miscellaneous
- Human Resources
- Recruitment
- Training
- Salaries and Wages
- Stationary
- Food
- Drinks
- Paper
- Folders
- Pen
- Printing
- Ink
- Maintenance
- Plumbing Repair
- Electrical Repair
- Utilities
- Electricity
- Water
- Taxes
- Plant Rental
- Cleaning Service

List absolutely everything that goes into your business. Grouping them under separate headings is one way to list everything so that you have a nice flow to your document, but each of these sections will still need to be expanded upon further to indicate separate line items. This is the only way to ensure you aren't missing anything on your cash flow projection.

Next to each item, indicate what you anticipate spending per month. There will be times when there are a lot of zeroes next to certain line items because you may not be at the point in your business where you need them. Also, if you happen to have budgeted for each of these items and the amount wasn't spent, this should normally be carried over to the following month.

The third section of the cash flow projection is reconciling your cash income and cash outflow.

Cash Flow Projection Reconciliation

Much in the same way that you reconciled your assets and liabilities in the previous section, here you would subtract what needs to be paid out against the funds coming into the business as a result of projected sales.

$$\text{Cash Outcome} - \text{Cash Income} = \text{Balance Projection}$$

This will then either leave you with a positive or negative balance (this is one of the most important figures necessary to make a decision on your business plan). Balances on this reconciliation are carried over to the following month.

Break-Even Analysis

The break-even analysis is the part of your financial plan that tells you how many items you need to sell in order to break-even. This analysis helps you in your costing when you need to know at what per-unit price you need to be selling your items at. It can also help you understand how many units you need to sell on a monthly basis to cover your operating costs. Your break-even point is when your costs and profits cancel each other out to zero. Breaking even means that you haven't made any profit as of yet.

Costing

The break-even analysis can help you with the actual costing out of your product before you even go to market. When costing your product, look at different percentages as profit margins to see how they affect your unit price and your break-even point. An example of this would be if your monthly fixed expenditure is $20,000 and your product price was currently $200 per unit. You would need to sell 100 units to break-even. However, if you altered your price to $250 per unit, your break-even point would only be 80 units per month.

While this is costing on one product, if you're working with more than one product, you would need to complete the same break-even analysis per product to give yourself a clearer picture of how many units you need to sell for you to cover your costs. Investors are especially interested in this information as it gives them a good sense of what volume of business you need to do to make a profit.

Markup

The break-even analysis also helps you understand what your markup, or the amount you need to add to a product to have a profit, needs to be. Given the above example, if you added the additional $50 to each unit price and you knew that your customer base would still pay this additional amount, you would already be making a profit of $5,000 if you achieved the 100 unit sales per month. Maybe the market isn't going to allow for the $50 increase and you need to be discounting the product by $50 instead. This would mean that 134 units was your break-even point instead and you would have no markup.

Variable Unit Cost

If you are currently sourcing a product from a wholesaler and rebranding and repackaging it to sell to the end user, depending on the quantities you order from your supplier and how quickly you pay them, you can potentially secure between a 10-15% markup on price. Your minimum order quantity is 500 units per month at a cost of $6 per unit. Each item costs you $10 to rebrand and repackage. Altogether, that would be a total expenditure of $8,000 for 500 rebranded and repackaged items. By selling each item for $17.60 (which a 10% markup), you would make a profit of $800.

Using Data

Using the information that you've already gathered during your market analysis, you should have a couple of ideas of various different price points that you can enter the market with and whether or not you can be aggressive with your pricing strategy. This is the part of your business plan where you need to be able to play with the information that you've found, and, as indicated in the two sections above, model various break-even price points per product that are within the high, medium, and low price range. This will allow investors to see that you've researched your market thoroughly, and you should be able to recognize whether your product is viable or not.

It's always in your best interest to be able to take your product to market at the highest price point. This makes the most logical sense in that you will break-even a lot quicker, make higher profit margins a lot quicker, and be able to repay investment loans a lot quicker.

Graphical Analysis

Your break-even analysis wouldn't really be an analysis without a section that can show where the different price breaks are. For example, you would take your sales volume and unit price and shift them to show different outcomes. A $5 upward shift upward would show a different break-even point than and $5 downward shift would. These shifts would then be related to how many units you would need to sell to meet a break-even point and a profit margin.

Place all of this information onto a spreadsheet that is visually appealing and either plot out the price breaks, use a bar graph, or employ a pie chart to show where your product needs to be positioned and how you are able to achieve the minimum and maximum numbers through your various distribution channels.

In closing, your financial plan is the brain of your entire business plan. You must present clear, concise information that is accurate and realistic. This part of your business plan will, ultimately, be the deciding factor for most potential investors. If your numbers are off or you don't flesh this section out enough, then you may just be on the receiving end of a rejection. Take your time with this section, gather your data and numbers, and ensure that you present your financials in a correct yet appealing manner.

Chapter 9: Appendices and Exhibits

> *"User experience is everything. It always has been, but it's undervalued and underinvested in. If you don't know user-centered design, study it. Hire people who know it. Obsess over it. Live it and breathe it. Get your whole company on board."*
>
> *~ Evan Williams, Co-Founder, Twitter*

This is the last section of the business plan that you will put together for your potential investors. Its purpose is to give them the overall look and feel of your business. It's where your entire business plan comes together and where you can showcase yourself and your business. This part of the plan gives you the opportunity to dazzle potential investors with the concept or idea that you've been dreaming about taking to market for so long.

Many don't believe that this final section is necessary; however, I think that it gives you an important platform. It can provide any and all potential investors or venture capitalists proof of all the claims made in your business plan so far. In the end, you will need to decide for yourself whether to include an appendix section or not. If you don't have a lot to include here or are sparse on documents, you may want to skip it. However, if you believe that the appendix section will really bolster you and act as a plus, then include it.

Because of the amount of information contained in this section, it is a rather bulky document. It may be worthwhile separating it from the actual business plan and creating a separate bound document. That way, a potential investor can choose for themselves whether they want to dive into it or not.

You can structure this document in such a way that it's easy for the reader to navigate. Just like the actual business plan document has an accurate and detailed table of contents, you may consider creating another table of contents for this section alone so that you make it simple and easy for anyone searching for a particular section to be able to do so without having to sift through a mountain of paperwork to find what they are looking for.

Occasionally, the reader is only interested in viewing certain documents and for them, the rest of the information that appears in this appendix section is purely icing on the cake. It's recommended that you place the most important documents right at the front of the appendix and work your way down from there to those items that have the least value or are less important for a financier to make a decision about whether or not to invest in your business.

Business Registration Documents

The first documents to include in your appendix section are all those that relate to your business registration. One of the first business tasks that you should have already completed was to register your business organization. There are a number of ways that you can go about this. You could either register a brand-new business or you may want to consider buying an off the shelf business organization that already has been registered but has never traded before.

Here, attach certified copies of all original business registration documents, taxation certificates, and any other documents of statutory compliance. You may need certificates of incorporation and/or other legal documents to be included here, too. If you have a certificate of affiliation to any other institution or body, this is where copies of these documents would go. An example of this would be if you are opening an accounting service, as you would need to be accredited and certified with national bodies. The same applies to real estate agencies.

Copies of Identity Documents of Business Owners and Shareholders

Here, attach certified copies of identity documents, such as a driver's license or birth certificate, of each of the business owners and/or shareholders. This is for investors to see that you are who you say you are. Investors may need all of your personal information to draw up loan documents. By providing all of this data here, it saves them having to ask you for it again later.

Credit History of Owners

You also want to include the credit histories, such as credit reports, of the business owners. It's important that investors can see that they're dealing with individuals who are honest and trustworthy and who are able to handle their money. After all, you're asking them to invest a fairly substantial amount into your business. Make certain that credit histories of all business owners are ready and available for perusal and scrutiny. Even if your credit track record isn't the best, whatever you do, don't try to hide it from investors. It's better to be honest and explain any reasons for bad credit and maybe include a plan for how you are actively improving your credit.

Bank Statements

If you have been operating already, provide bank statements as far back as you can go (to a maximum of 12 months). This will give investors a feel for what you've already been able to achieve on your own to date. They will also recognize any specific trends in your banking history, which could, in turn, indicate trends in what's happening in the marketplace.

Banking Information

If you have not traded before, you should at least have opened a bank account under the company name. Provide all of this information here. The financial institution should be one that is reputable and experienced in working with business organizations.

Accountants Information

You also want to provide information about your accountants of record. This is important as your account will be signing off your books annually and managing your taxes. Investors want to know that you are working with reputable individuals.

Attorneys Information

Like your accountants, you want to provide detailed information on your attorneys. They will be responsible for drawing up any and all agreements from partnership agreements to any special financial agreements with independent financiers.

Resumes

It is important that potential investors see that you have the qualifications necessary to run a business. Whether you've just graduated from business school or you're a seasoned professional who's been around the block a few times, highlight specific parts of your career on your resume that you believe to be important when looking to finance a new business. This could be past experience running a business or specific ventures you were a part of. Additionally, ensure that you include the professional resumes of everyone that you are planning on bringing into the business from the start. If you are currently working with third parties, it may be helpful to be able to provide a brief overview of their business, the business owners, and why you've chosen to be working alongside them in the first place.

Copies of Existing Agreements

You should attach copies of any and all agreements you have signed to date. If you've signed rental agreements for office space (or you're considering signing) or if you have signed agreements with other business partners, attach copies of each of these agreements here. This may include lease agreements for vehicles, office equipment rentals, such as copiers or switchboards, and any other agreements that you're considering for the business.

Financial Information

All relevant financial information that was discussed in your business plan needs to be inserted here. This could include anything from your lists of assets and liabilities to your income statements. You also want to attach your balance sheet, if you have one.

Forecasting documents where you've done all your calculations can also be included here for perusal by potential investors.

Building Office Plans

If you've already found suitable space that could be used for offices, it's vital to secure a copy of the office plans so that you can map out your business before you purchase one item of furniture or buy that potted plant that you know will look perfect in the reception area. Even if you're leasing space, office plans should be available via the building management. Insist on acquiring a copy of these so you can keep these on record and not just as a matter of strengthening your business plan. It will prove invaluable to you when it comes to deciding on office space, storage space, and whether your offices comply with all regulatory health and safety standards.

Letters of Recommendation

Referrals are also known as letters of recommendation, and the more of these you're able to ask for and gather, the greater your chance of securing finance for your business will be. These referrals or recommendations can come from anyone who has done business with you in the past. Never be shy in asking for a recommendation from a former boss or partner. It's beneficial to you if they can refer to your business experience, your skill, your knowledge, your character, and your shared successes.

Patents, Trademarks, and Design Registrations

If you have received or are in the process of working toward any patents, trademarks, or design registrations, you want to include copies of them here. If you haven't been granted them yet, you can include your applications. If you are in the very early stages of this process, you could even include the names of potential patent or trademark attorneys with some indicative prices so that those who are possibly looking into financing your business organization will have some figures and/or information to work from.

Marketing Analysis

Whatever marketing reports and marketing analysis you've conducted can be included in this specific section. One example of a marketing document that you could include is that SWOT analysis you completed way back in the market analysis and competition chapter of this book. You might also include any reports about market trends, your competition, your social media strategy, and your overall marketing strategy.

Information on Products

The section about your products will prove to be one of the largest sections in this appendix document. You should look at including as many pictures of your products as you can, even if your products are still only in the design stage. Further, make sure to include size dimensions, color variations, unique details, and printing and packaging information. If you are a service-based business, then add a detailed description of what your service is. Simplified examples would be explaining the process of the training seminars you will be offering or describing what types of accounting services you will be offering.

Links to Website

If you have a website and are using other social media marketing platforms, such as Facebook, Instagram, Twitter, Pinterest, or LinkedIn, provide the links to them here. You want to demonstrate to investors that you already have a web presence and are building your brand. Also, be sure to add these as hyperlinks to make it easier for potential investors to click on the link when you are forwarding any of this information via email or in an electronic format.

Brochures or Other Marketing Material Already Produced

By including any brochures, flyers, or other marketing materials that you've already produced, you can easily share your vision for your brand and your product directly with your potential investors or financiers. This is important because you want to give them a taste of what your business or brand will be about. You can also demonstrate that you are thinking big picture in terms of developing your brand and marketing it.

If you've already settled on a name and have a logo for your business, include it here and show examples of how it will be used on letterhead, on ads, or on promotional items. When it comes to your products and/or services, you can showcase your designs and brand names here as well by including photographs of your branded products. My recommendation is to stick with the basics and designs that are simple and memorable. Avoid choosing colors that are currently popular but may have a short shelf life or lifespan. When choosing logos for branded products, look at what others in your industry have done but follow your own path. Remember that less is more, especially when it comes to marketing and advertising. Follow the trends of major brands, and you will notice that if ever they change, it's only fine tweaks that happen. Your marketing materials should have a timeless feel yet should also be reflective of your product or service.

Trade Agreements

You need to include copies of any and all trade agreements that you've managed to secure so far in your business dealings. You may have secured listings with some major retailers, such as Costco or Walmart. Maybe they've agreed to stock your product in one or two stores to see how it goes at first, but you have high hopes for being in more stores. This type of agreement is something that you are going to want to showcase here as it proves your product is desirable and you have the skills needed to broker such deals. Include copies of these trade agreements in this section so that potential investors can see that you've already secured some orders on your own and the business has potential without their investment. This may also mean that their investment doesn't need to be as large as previously anticipated or they may be prepared to sponsor you on a monthly basis for a fixed duration.

Quotes or Copies of Mortgage, Loans Docs, and Leases

You've almost compiled everything you need for your appendix section, but you also need to include copies of all the quotes on leases, loans, and any other business expenditure documents that you've collected thus far. These could be anything from brochures advertising office furniture to quotes for computers and IT installation. If you have viewed multiple possible offices to work out of include lease information for each one here, too. If you have already signed any agreements that are currently in place, include certified copies of each of these documents here so that financiers know the duration of those agreements. This gives them the opportunity to either buyout the existing agreement or allow the agreement to run its natural course. If you have taken out any loans for your business, include them as well. You may be shopping around for loans as well, so also include any loan application you've filled out, too.

Other Supporting Material for First Impression

Whatever other supporting material you may think will make a good first impression should be included as part of this appendix in this last section. Usually, this will be any documentation that doesn't precisely fit in other sections. This may include things like your letterhead, business cards, sample packaging, or sample material if you are offering a service rather than a product. For example, a beauty salon business might include its service offerings and price list that has already been designed and printed on high-quality paper.

Include anything else that you believe may be relevant for potential investors to make a buy-in decision. This document is like a monumental sales pitch, but all on paper, so ensure that you are providing proof that you and your business already have a ton of value.

Conclusion

"Every minute you spend in planning saves 10 minutes in execution; this gives you a 1,000 percent return on energy!"

~ Brian Tracy, Author and Motivational Speaker

Up to this point, you have described all the ins and outs of your business and know what should or shouldn't be included as part of your business plan document and its appendix. In business, you should be looking toward one goal and one goal only: Creating an awareness around your business and industry in order to secure new business opportunities for yourself and to grow your brand. Your smaller goals need to be aligned and should feed into that one larger goal.

Remember that it's your business and you alone know what your ultimate plans are and where exactly you want your business to be in the future. While the main goal of this document is to attract financial assistance from a venture capitalist, angel investor, financier, or business partner, the details of your business should remain in your court.

There are a number of things that are extremely important when it comes to working with investors and these are the following:

1. Don't settle for the first person that comes along.
2. You have a right to choose who you want to be in business with.
3. Do your own homework to ensure the partnership or business relationship is going to work for you.
4. Remember that the business ideas belong to you, and you need to protect this information at all costs.

Entering into a business partnership with a venture capitalist or financier is like entering into a marriage. It's going to be a lengthy relationship, and you must be able to trust one another, respect one another, and most important of all, be able to work together seamlessly. If you each are pulling in different directions, this alliance can never work. You need to look for any differences that could result in a business implosion before signing onto anything.

When signing agreements with financiers, take time to go through all of the documentations and study the fine print. Be certain that there are benefits for both parties but also that there's a get-out clause for both of you should the relationship not work like you would've wanted it to.

Remember the experience I had when partners refused to put their money where their mouths were? It cost 2 years of potential earnings that could have gone back into the business rather than being paid out as director's salaries and expenses. This was a huge mistake that I had to learn the hard way.

Unfortunately, in life and in business, most people are out just for themselves. Trust no one unless you have the agreement in writing in front of you. Even so, have your attorneys investigate the documents to ensure that they are legitimate, legal, and fair for all parties concerned. If there are any clauses included in the agreement that you're not sure about, either ask your attorneys or the financiers to explain it until you do understand.

When taking on a partner or investor, know what you and your business are getting into. If you are about to sign a deal with a venture capitalist, do your own homework on them. If they're worth their salt, they should have a rather lengthy track record of victories and failures—and yes, you heard me correctly! One of the most important characteristics of all successful venture capitalists (and most successful individuals, for that matter) is that they often lose as much as they win.

The venture capitalist I learned from had anywhere between 15 to 20 other companies that he was running simultaneously, which meant he would often lose as much money as he made. Not that any of this phased him too much, because he was aware that markets have trends that continue to go up and down. He understood the world of business and how it worked, and he wasn't afraid to take chances on those around him. If someone approached him with an idea that he was certain could make him enough money, he would entertain them and hear them out. Not that he would always invest in each of these schemes, but he was never rude to people or condescending when it came to business ideas. He had learned over his years as an entrepreneur, businessman, and venture capitalist that there's always something that can be salvaged and turned into a winning combination. And that's something you should consider, too. Maybe your business idea isn't the best it can be now, but there's something in there you can build on.

As we've worked through this book, there have been a number of key takeaways from each chapter that I'd like to highlight here.

Your Business Plan and Protecting Your Ideas

Crafting your business plan is one of the most important things that you will ever do in preparation to getting your business to market. This will tell you whether you have an idea that's worth pursuing or not. Although some might think you don't need one, I think we've established that you do because the benefits of creating a business plan are endless. It will help lay the foundation for your future success. Your business plan is a document that you can use to find financing, convince investors to work with you, and act as a blueprint for how you will run your business.

When you are at the stage of beginning negotiations with anyone who may be interested in hopping on board with you, ensure that you plan on having an NDA in place that they can sign before mentioning the first thing about your business. This is important to protect your business ideas or intellectual property. You probably have a lot of sweat equity invested in your business, so it would be a shame to lose your business or ideas because you weren't vigilant. Remember that people can be totally unscrupulous and dishonest. Until there's mutual respect, trust no one. Financiers, venture capitalists, and angel investors are used to signing NDAs, so this will be nothing new to them. As a matter of fact, they may have one of their own for you to sign.

Executive Summary, Product and/or Service, Customer Base, Competition, and Financing

The first part of your business plan is your executive summary. Along with your financial plan, your executive summary is one of the most important parts of your business plan. In this section, you should take a sweeping overview of your business, covering the key parts, such as your mission statement, who your management team is, and what your market opportunities are. You should also include brief notes about your place in the market and what your competitive advantage is. This section also needs to include financial projections. Think of your executive summary as an "elevator pitch," by which I mean it should be short enough that you could tell it to another person in the span of time it takes to enter an elevator and travel up a few floors. Whoever is reading your executive summary wants to quickly know all the key points of your business so that they can decide if they want to read further.

After this section, you will dive into other sections that center on describing your product and/or service in-depth. Further, you will include a section that gives an overview of your intended customer base and who your competition is in the marketplace. Last, you will have a section that gives a brief introduction to your financing goals and plans. You might even include a detailed budget of your startup costs.

Clearly Define Your Business and the Nature of Industry

The business overview section of your business plan should be a detailed outline of your business that goes deeper than your executive summary. You also want to be sure that you include the reason for doing what you are doing. This part of your business plan should scream passion, dedication, hard work, and commitment. If that's not the message that's being delivered by this section, then you've missed the point of the narrative. Although much of this section involves the ins and outs of your potential business operation, you may want to spend a fair amount of time making certain that you've accurately pinpointed why you want to pursue this business in the first place. Any signs of insecurity in this part of your business plan will result in investors chewing you up and spitting you out. Remember that this section is where you clearly define your "why" behind your business. Whether you're doing it to save others time and money or you're passionate about customer service, whatever the reason, make certain that it's clearly communicated in this part of your business plan.

Next, your nature of industry section should be a deep dive into all aspects of the industry and marketplace you are entering in. Include details and insights into current trends, target customers, and your existing competition. This section should show potential investors that you know each and every part, no matter how small, of your marketplace and your place in it.

Market Analysis

Your market analysis section should be thorough and detailed, and the numbers should be a true reflection of what's happening in your business and in the marketplace. Going to market with false data could damage your brand and create unnecessary barriers to enter the marketplace. Remember that this is where you're going to want to use a SWOT analysis to provide you with most of the information you need. Be as honest as possible with this SWOT analysis rather than using this tool loosely or not using it at all. It can be a powerful resource in identifying where your market really is. It may also uncover potential opportunities that you hadn't even considered up until this point in your business plan.

Sales and Marketing Plan

Your sales and marketing section is going to provide you and your possible investors with a clear picture of where and how you can position your product in the marketplace, which will be based on some of the market intelligence you've already gathered. This section will help you accurately price your products and services and will include sales forecasts that work to strategically align your business goals and your sales and marketing plan. Consider all the things needed for the perfect marketing mix and work toward common business goals to achieve your sales and marketing targets. In this section of your business plan, you should be able to work according to marketing's 4 P's: product, position, price, and promotion. While these may seem to be simple, working from this foundation can successfully position your product where you need it to be, including having the right price, targeting the right market, and promoting it in the right way.

Management Plan

The most important takeaway from the management plan section is that you should be able to clearly define how your business organization is going to be structured. You need to be clear about who is going to take on which role in managing the business. This also provides a clear guideline as to all business relationships, not only within the organization but also with third-party service providers and vendors.

Operating Plan

The operating plan outlines the day-to-day operations of your business. A clear operating plan also allows your business to achieve specific strategic objectives by working together as a cohesive team. It's important to understand how all the pieces of the puzzle fit together to create an organization that operates like a well-oiled machine. Initially, this would involve a much smaller workforce. Your operating plan would provide timelines and dates to indicate growth within the business and how additional departments and key personnel might be added.

Financial Plan

The financial plan is of the utmost importance as it can either convince a financier to get involved in your business or not. They should be able to get a quick glimpse at the figures for the business, which will tell them all that they need to know to decide to either invest with you or not.

Ensure that all the information provided here is accurate and up to date. Be honest with the numbers in your financial plan. Financiers will analyze and weigh this information to determine whether or not your business plan is a good investment or the right investment for them. Investors have probably been crunching numbers a lot longer than you have, so respect their judgment. If they come back to you after studying this section of your business plan with a negative response, whatever you do, don't throw a tantrum. Thank them for their time and patience in meeting with you, and you may even want to ask them who they know that may be interested. Never underestimate the power of connections. These people are all very well-connected and know one another. You may even want to keep updating this section of your business plan with new numbers and insights as well.

Final Thoughts

I know embarking on the process of writing a business plan can be intimidating and stressful, but with this book, you have a good guide about how to get started and where you need to go. Having spent nearly four decades in the business world, I've been lucky enough to have been tutored in the art of business plans by many great business people. Without them, I wouldn't be where I am today.

It's time to hand the torch over to you so you can benefit through shared knowledge. There's a whole world out there that's simply waiting for small businesses and entrepreneurs to take their rightful place in the marketplace. Don't be afraid to step out of your comfort zone and give it a try. There's an old saying that goes "nothing ventured, nothing gained." What that means for you is that it's time for you to turn your dream business idea into a reality. After all, if you don't venture forth with it, you'll never know where exactly it can take you.

Now that you have all of this information in one place, I trust that you will refer to it often. You've been given an entire working career's worth of trial and error and expertise all neatly arranged into chapters and sections that you can come back to as you work on your business plan. I want to be part of your success story, which is why I've spent so much time compiling this work for you! Don't let that great idea slip through your fingers for one more instant. You know that you can be successful, and you now have the tools to help you determine which of your ideas are surefire winners and which are maybe still ahead of their time.

Use that entrepreneurial spirit for good. You and you alone hold the power of change in your own hands. You can either continue along the same boring path that you've been trudging along or you can step out of the shadows and take a chance on the dreams that have been part of you for as long as you can remember. All that remains is to ask yourself how badly you want to enjoy entrepreneurial success in your life. Do you want to achieve what you were born to achieve? I know that the answer is "yes." So, what are you waiting for? This book contains the roadmap to your success, and all you need to do is follow it.

References

Adams, R. L. (2017). *10 marketing strategies to fuel your business growth.* Entrepreneur. https://www.entrepreneur.com/article/299335

Ameet Ranadive. (2017, May 26). *The power of starting with why.* Medium; Leadership. https://medium.com/leadership-motivation-and-impact/the-power-of-starting-with-why-f8e491392ef8

Bezos, J. (2020, July 28). *Statement by Jeff Bezos to the U.S. House Committee on the Judiciary.* US Day One Blog. https://blog.aboutamazon.com/policy/statement-by-jeff-bezos-to-the-u-s-house-committee-on-the-judiciary

Biography.com Editors. (2017, April 28). *Mary Kay Ash Biography.* Biography. https://www.biography.com/business-figure/mary-kay-ash

Boudreau, D. (2013, March 14). *Seven attachments that make your business plan more credible | Business plan oasis.* Riskbuster.Com. http://www.riskbuster.com/seven-attachments-that-make-your-business-plan-more-credible/

Bradley, J. (2012). *Sales plan vs. Marketing plan.* Chron.Com. https://smallbusiness.chron.com/sales-plan-vs-marketing-plan-57267.html

Breschi, A. (2019). *16 Types of customer needs (and how to solve for them).* Hubspot.Com. https://blog.hubspot.com/service/customer-needs

Covey, S. R. (2020). *7 Habits of highly effective people: Revised and updated.* Simon & Schuster Ltd. (Original work published 1989)

Cremades, A. (2018, September 11). *How to create A business plan.* Forbes. https://www.forbes.com/sites/alejandrocremades/2018/07/24/how-to-create-a-business-plan/

Definitions from Oxford Languages. (2020). business plan. In *Oxford.*

Elliott, T. (2019). *10 Steps to an effective marketing strategy.* The Balance Small Business. https://www.thebalancesmb.com/creating-a-sales-and-marketing-strategy-2947172

Entrepreneur. (2019a). *Business plan definition - Entrepreneur small business encyclopedia.* Entrepreneur. https://www.entrepreneur.com/encyclopedia/business-plan

Entrepreneur. (2019b). *Competitive Analysis definition - Entrepreneur small business encyclopedia.* Entrepreneur. https://www.entrepreneur.com/encyclopedia/competitive-analysis

Entrepreneur. (2019c). *Mission statement definition - Entrepreneur small business encyclopedia.* Entrepreneur. https://www.entrepreneur.com/encyclopedia/mission-statement

Entrepreneur.com. (2019). *Elements of a business plan.* Entrepreneur. https://www.entrepreneur.com/article/38308

Fersht, P. (2020, August 8). *You've got to start with the customer experience and work backwards to the technology.* Horses for Sources. https://www.horsesforsources.com/steve-jobs1997_080820

Forbes. (2020). *America's most innovative leaders.* Forbes. https://www.forbes.com/lists/innovative-leaders/#28c02f7b26aa

Friedman, J. (2018, August 21). *Top 15 financial planning quotes that will inspire you.* Millionaire Mob. https://millionairemob.com/financial-planning-quotes/

Frost, A. (2019). *The ultimate guide to sales forecasting.* Hubspot.Com. https://blog.hubspot.com/sales/sales-forecasting

Haden, J. (2015, April 9). *How to write a great business plan: Competitive analysis.* Inc.Com; Inc. https://www.inc.com/jeff-haden/how-to-write-a-great-business-plan-competitive-analysis.html

Haden, J. (2016, December 13). *Want to be super successful? Science says do any 1 of these 10 things.* Inc.Com; Inc. https://www.inc.com/jeff-haden/want-to-be-super-successful-science-says-do-any-1-of-these-10-things.html

Haden, J. (2018, July 20). *How to write the perfect business plan: A comprehensive guide.* Inc.Com; Inc. https://www.inc.com/jeff-haden/how-to-write-perfect-business-plan-a-comprehensive-guide.html

Hansen, D. (2013, December 20). Myth busted: Steve Jobs did listen to customers. *Forbes.* https://www.forbes.com/sites/drewhansen/2013/12/19/myth-busted-steve-jobs-did-listen-to-customers/

Marketing MO. (2018, April 7). *Strategic planning - How to develop your distribution channels.* Marketing MO. http://www.marketingmo.com/strategic-planning/how-to-develop-your-distribution-channels/

Markgraf, B. (n.d.). *Distribution methods and marketing plans.* Smallbusiness.Chron.Com. https://smallbusiness.chron.com/distribution-methods-marketing-plans-60788.html

McNaught, D. (2018). *What supporting documents should you attach to your business plan?* All Business Technologies. https://www.allbusiness.com/what-supporting-documents-should-you-attach-to-your-business-plan-1742-1.html

Mishra, S. (n.d.). *How to write a financial section for your startup business plan?* Upmetrics. https://upmetrics.co/blog/write-financial-section-startup-business-plan

Moskowitz, C. (2008, April 28). *Mind's limit found: 4 Things at once.* Livescience.Com; Live Science. https://www.livescience.com/2493-mind-limit-4.html

Murray, J. (2019, May 9). *5 Easy steps to creating a break-even analysis.* The Balance Small Business. https://www.thebalancesmb.com/how-to-do-a-break-even-analysis-398032

Peek, S. (2019, December 23). *How to write a business plan - Business News Daily.* Www.Businessnewsdaily.Com. https://www.businessnewsdaily.com/4533-business-plan-outline.html

Prince, A. (2014, November 5). *15 inspiring college dropouts who prove hard work is the way to success.* Lifehack. https://www.lifehack.org/articles/productivity/15-inspiring-college-dropouts-who-prove-hard-work-the-way-success.html

Pogue, S. (2019, March 7). *45 Powerful planning quotes to help you reach your goals.* Workzone. https://www.workzone.com/blog/project-planning-quotes/

Rampton, J. (2019). *7 Steps to a perfectly written business plan.* Entrepreneur. https://www.entrepreneur.com/article/281416

Shrodt, P. (2017, November 11). *15 Incredibly successful people who never graduated from college.* Business Insider. https://www.businessinsider.com/15-incredibly-successful-people-who-never-graduated-from-college-2017-11?amp

Sinek, S. (2013). *Start with why : how great leaders inspire everyone to take action.* Portfolio/Penguin. (Original work published 2009)

Spacey, J. (2019). *4 Examples of an operations plan.* Simplicable. https://simplicable.com/new/operations-plan

Staff of Entrepreneur Media Inc. (2015, January 4). *First steps: Writing the management section of your business plan*. Entrepreneur. https://www.entrepreneur.com/article/241072

Stowers, J. (2020, February 6). *How to write a financial business plan*. Www.Businessnewsdaily.Com. https://www.businessnewsdaily.com/10644-write-financial-section-business-plan.html

Strategyn. (2019). *Customer needs | Analysis and assessment | Strategyn*. Strategyn. https://strategyn.com/outcome-driven-innovation-process/customer-needs/

Travis, D. (2018, March 5). *Steve Jobs on 6 key principles of user experience*. Www.Userfocus.Co.Uk. https://www.userfocus.co.uk/articles/Steve-Jobs-on-6-key-principles-of-ux.html

Ward, S. (2018a). *Business Plan tips: How to write the competitor analysis section*. The Balance Small Business. https://www.thebalancesmb.com/how-to-write-the-competitive-analysis-section-of-the-business-plan-2947025

Ward, S. (2018b). *Every business needs sales forecasting - Here's how to do it*. The Balance Small Business. https://www.thebalancesmb.com/sales-forecasting-2948317

Ward, S. (2019a). *How to write the management plan section of your business plan*. The Balance Small Business. https://www.thebalancesmb.com/management-section-of-business-plan-2947028

Ward, S. (2019b, October 7). *Business plan essentials: Writing a cash flow projection*. The Balance Small Business. https://www.thebalancesmb.com/writing-the-business-plan-section-8-2947026

Ward, S. (2019c, December 9). *Writing an operations plan for your business*. The Balance Small Business. https://www.thebalancesmb.com/operating-section-or-business-plan-2947031

Wasserman, E. (2018). *How to write the financial section of a business plan*. Inc.Com; Inc. https://www.inc.com/guides/business-plan-financial-section.html

White, C. (2018). *What's a competitive analysis & how do you conduct one?* Hubspot.Com. https://blog.hubspot.com/marketing/competitive-analysis-kit

Wroblewski, M. T. (2019, April 26). *What is an appendix in a business plan?* Small Business - Chron.Com. https://smallbusiness.chron.com/appendix-business-plan-11090.html

www.ingramcontent.com/pod-product-compliance
Lightning Source LLC
Chambersburg PA
CBHW060851220526
45466CB00003B/1332